The Ecclesial Cr

Appreciation f

It becomes manifestly clear that Metropolitan Nikiforos, in a spirit of the love of Christ, is deeply concerned for the necessary cooperation and concord among the Orthodox.

+TIMOTHEOS, Metropolitan of Bostra
Patriarchate of Jerusalem

This situation in which we Orthodox have found ourselves is completely unnatural and does not serve the good of the Orthodox Church, rather it is contrary to it. We pray to the Almighty God and the Most-Holy Theotokos that this division ends quickly and Church order will reign again. We are pleased that writings such as this work by Metropolitan Nikiforos are working towards this correction.

+LONGIN, Bishop of New Gracanica and Midwestern America,
Patriarchate of Serbia

This book addresses the many arguments and ways towards unity and the common Orthodox Church in Ukraine focused on serving God and His faithful. This lively analysis presents the situation of the Orthodox Church in Ukraine in an accessible way to both theologians, the faithful, and all people interested in the topic of the unity of the Orthodox Church in Ukraine.

+ABEL, Archbishop of Lublin and Chelm,
Orthodox Church of Poland

This is a serious study of a crisis in the life of our Orthodox Church worldwide that deserves to be widely read as we seek to understand the underlying issues more clearly and find a conciliar solution that brings both unity and peace.

+JURAJ, Archbishop of Michalovce and Košice
Orthodox Church of the Czech Lands and Slovakia

The
Ecclesial Crisis
in Ukraine

and its Solution According to the Sacred Canons

By Metropolitan Nikiforos
of Kykkos and Tylliria, Cyprus

Translated by Holy Trinity Monastery

Holy Trinity Publications
Holy Trinity Seminary Press
Holy Trinity Monastery
Jordanville, New York

2021

HOLY TRINITY
SEMINARY PRESS

An imprint of

HOLY TRINITY PUBLICATIONS
Holy Trinity Monastery
Jordanville, New York 13361-0036
www.holytrinitypublications.com

ISBN: 978-1-942699-41-5 (paperback)
ISBN: 978-1-942699-44-6 (ePub)
ISBN: 978-1-942699-45-3 (Mobi/Kindle)

Library of Congress Control Number 2021936699

Cover Photo: "The Kiev Pechersk Lavra" by tverkhovinets.
Source: stock.adobe.com. 53815043

Originally published in Greek: Το σύγχρονο Ουκρανικό ζήτημα και η κατά
τους θείους και ιερούς κανόνες επίλυσή του
(The Contemporary Ukraine Question and Its Solution According to the
Divine and Sacred Canons by His Eminence Metropolitan of Kykkos and
Tylliria Nikiforos, Cyprus) © 2020
ΚΕΝΤΡΟ ΜΕΛΕΤΩΝ ΙΕΡΑΣ ΜΟΝΗΣ ΚΥΚΚΟΥ
Τ.Θ. 28192, 2093 ΛΕΥΚΩΣΙΑ, ΚΥΠΡΟΣ
ISBN: 978-9963-253-35-7

Contents

Foreword

"For Zion's sake I will not be silent, and for Jerusalem's sake I will not rest, until my righteousness goes forth as light, and my salvation burns like a lamp." (Isaiah 62:1)

We are thankful to God for the opportunity to give a voice in the English language to a Bishop of the ancient and venerable Church of Cyprus, founded by the apostle St Barnabas, co-worker of the apostle St Paul. Metropolitan Nikiforos's words demand careful reading and attention: they have been penned in the context of the ongoing crisis set upon the Orthodox Church by the actions of the Ecumenical Patriarchate with regard to Ukraine in 2018. But even beyond addressing this, they speak to the heart of what it means to be the Body of Christ, and how we must relate one to another at all times. The Church must manifest both its hierarchical and conciliar aspects if the Gospel is to be preached to all nations as our Lord and Saviour Jesus Christ commanded.

As the Metropolitan writes, it is essential that the "Ecclesiastical Conscience" of all believers be aroused and an understanding gained of what is at issue in this dispute centered in Ukraine. This crisis is not as the secular media portray it, a question of the political aspirations of secular governments clashing over power and control. It is first and foremost an ecclesial crisis whose remedy must lie with repentance: a turning around from where our sins have led us to a reaffirmation of mutual love and submission one to another. We must constantly remain mindful that in the Kingdom of Christ "the last will be first, and the first last" (Matthew 20:16).

We commend this work to your prayerful and attentive reading.

Holy Trinity Monastery
Great Lent 2021

The Synaxis of Primates of the Orthodox Autocephalous Churches that took place at the Orthodox Center of the Ecumenical Patriarchate in Chambésy, Geneva from 21–28 January 2016. His All-Holiness the Ecumenical Patriarch Bartholomew is seen seated in the middle of the front row. One row behind him, two places to his right and wearing a white hat is Metropolitan Onufry of Kiev and All Ukraine, universally recognized at this time as the canonical head of the Ukrainian Orthodox Church. Less than three years after this, the eumenical patriarch would unilaterally set up an alternative ecclesiastical structure in Ukraine based around two groups that up until then were considered schismatic by all the churches gathered in Chambésy in 2016.

Preface
to the Greek Language Edition

No one can deny the fact that the universal Orthodox Church currently finds herself in a state of divisive crisis due to the Ukrainian ecclesiastical issue, which was created by the Ecumenical Patriarchate of Constantinople's unilateral and anti-canonical grant of autocephaly to schismatic elements of the Ukrainian Church, without the knowledge of the Russian Orthodox Patriarchate, which is the Mother Church of the Orthodox ecclesiastical eparchy in Ukraine. In recent years, the Ukrainian issue has been at the center of contemporary Orthodox concerns, with endless discussions, arguments, and counter-arguments from both sides, a fact which is causing fissures in the unity of the pan-Orthodox Church.

For the last few months I have been debating whether I should remain immersed in my silence, or write and express my anguish and opinion on this burning topic.

The voice of my hierarchal conscience resounded urgently within me: "You must overcome your hesitations. You must emerge from your defeatist indolence and comfortable passivity. You must actively engage—in writing—with this issue because, to quote the Latin proverb, *verba volant scripta manent*[1] (what is spoken flies away, what is written remains)." In the end, the consciousness of my responsibility and obligation to the unity of the Orthodox Church did not allow me to remain shrewdly neutral, a colorless, indifferent, listless, and complacent bishop. Moved, then, out of fear that God might hold us partly culpable, responsible for our silence on such a dramatic issue which threatens to divide universal Orthodoxy, I began, timidly conscious of an urgent obligation, to research and write about this complex issue. I started in November of 2019, but over the course of my research, various cares (pastoral work, administration, financial management, cultural, charitable, social, and other activities) prevented me from continuing the present study, and at other times even threatened to put a complete stop to it.

Amidst these difficulties, upheavals, and vacillations, there suddenly came the great trial of the coronavirus epidemic, which was accompanied by a painful and distressing forced isolation, which reached borderline tragic dimensions. However, this isolation and loneliness freed me from the world and its daily cares, and gave me the opportunity to more deeply reexamine my present scholarly undertaking, and to start writing, humbly conscious of my limitations, the following book. When the compulsory isolation due to the difficult existential trial of the coronavirus pandemic got particularly oppressive, I was given the opportunity to "lay aside all earthly cares,"[2] and, without the panicked fear of death which hovered in the atmosphere, to throw myself with divine passion into researching and writing this small treatise.

The nearly three months of compulsory isolation were, for me, the most spiritually fruitful and productive. In situations like this "you justly remember … the old sayings 'there is no evil unmixed with good' and 'from the bitter emerges the sweet.'[3]

This simple, humble book has no other ambition but to give the Orthodox faithful who live in the "fear" and "shadow"[4] of a catastrophic schism in Orthodoxy information on the necessary elements which make up the Ukrainian Ecclesiastical issue. It can help readers form a full and correct opinion, according to the sacred canonical tradition of the Orthodox Church, and so to be led to the appropriate behavior. I believe that every believer, every spiritual, religious individual is obliged to know the truth of the matter if they wish to evaluate it correctly. Otherwise, they will have the hazy, blurred, distorted image of the problem, which biased, subjective dissenters will make sure to present to them.

The basic issue which will occupy us in this book is whether autocephaly was rightly or wrongly granted to Ukraine. This study seeks, without subterfuge or ulterior motives, to provide the reader with the necessary elements which make up the Ukrainian issue. It does not seek to embellish or dramatize, but rather to present the truth impersonally. That is, without prejudice, sympathy, or antipathy. I write, to quote the holy Apostle, from "sincerity … as from God, we speak in the sight of God in Christ."[5]

In my humble endeavor to adequately develop the topic, I will proceed on the basis of the sacred canons of the ecumenical councils, the canons of local councils of ecumenical standing, the canons of the God-bearing fathers, and the relevant bibliography and subject matter. When the need arises, we will also cite the word of God, enshrined in the Holy Scriptures (Old and New Testaments).

My writing about the Ukrainian issue, which is a heated and complicated matter, is not for personal reasons. I am doing it for reasons of conscience and consequences, fully aware of the potential misunderstandings and dangers that the endeavor entails. It is highly likely that the objective development of this topic will arouse reactions. It is possible that this book will incite polemics from intolerant nationalists and other distorters of the truth. It is possible that by publishing this small work I am provoking the thunderbolts to strike me personally. The arrows of deceitful critique and the mud of slander may be turned at me. "Enemies and treacherous plotters,"[6] both visible and invisible, may seek my harm.

I am aware that one who seeks the truth and has the courage to proclaim it is always temporarily afflicted. But I am likewise aware that "Christian hope always looks beyond Calvary to the luminous reflections of the glorious Resurrection. The triumph of evil is always temporary."[7]

So, in this case, if it happens that opponents muster all audacity and shamelessness to malign and try to demolish me, then I will be comforted and strengthened by the words of the Apostle Peter: "If you are reproached for the name of Christ, blessed are you … "[8] Above all, however, I will be comforted by the words of the Lord Himself, in His Sermon on the Mount: "Blessed are you when they revile and persecute you, and say all kinds of evil against you falsely for My sake."[9] Bearing all these things in mind, I will say with the Psalmist: "Yea, though I walk through the valley of the shadow of death, I will fear no evil, for Thou art with me."[10] I await not the praise of men, but the glory of heaven.

Before concluding the preface of this present study, I consider it a necessary duty to publicly express my gratitude to my distinguished associates for their selflessness and diligence, and the work to which they subjected themselves in order to make the publication of the present work possible. The work at hand received its definitive content and final form thanks to valuable contributions, suggestions, and useful linguistic corrections from the Director of the Ecclesiastical Ministry of the Holy Metropolis of Kykkos and Tylliria, Professor Emeritus at the University of Athens, and Professor at the University of Nicosia, Nikos Nikolaidis, as well as the kind, substantial contribution and invaluable assistance of our excellent associates: Voula Papandreou, my personal secretary; Kostas Kokkinoftas, Director of the Holy Monastery of Kykkos Research Center; and protopresbyter Paraskevas Papamihail, Director of the metropolis office, each of whom, with commendable eagerness, offered what they could. Their cooperation was very important. I would also like to thank the Holy Monastery of Kykkos Research Center for the special honor of including this small treatise, which does not claim scientific comprehensiveness, in its series of weighty publications. I also express my gratitude to R.P.M. Lithographica Printers for the proper technical and artistic layout of this book, and more generally for the aesthetic beauty of its impeccable typographical appearance.

In concluding this preface, I give thanks and praise from the depths of my soul to "my God through Jesus Christ,"[11] who made me worthy to complete the present study, which I offer, as the least gift in return, to Him and to the holy plenitude of His church.

I submit this publication to the indulgence and prayers of godly readers, with ardent prayers to the Almighty and Good Lord, that He may grant wisdom and comprehension to all.

September 8, 2020

Feast of the Most Holy Theotokos Eleousa of Kykkos

Metropolitan of Kykkos and Tillyria, Nikiforos

Introduction

The present work is the result of intense anxiety and great anguish over what is currently happening regarding the ecclesiastical issues in our dearest, fellow-Orthodox country of Ukraine, due to Ecumenical Patriarch Bartholomew's recent grant of autocephaly (without the knowledge or consent of the other Orthodox Autocephalous Churches) to two anticanonical, schismatic elements of the Ukrainian church: Filaret Denisenko, who was excommunicated and anathematized by the Holy Synod of the Church of Russia, and the self-ordained (unordained) Makary Maletich.

The purpose of this study is twofold; first, to inform the Christian flock of the most holy Church of Cyprus. They have shown deep interest in what is taking place in Ukraine, while concurrently expressing fears for wider Orthodoxy, hoping and praying that the unresolved Ukrainian ecclesiastical issue does not spread through the entire body of universal Orthodoxy, with all the tragedy and devastation that this implies. Second, in a spirit of humility and kenotic love, to more fully inform, as much as possible, my beloved brothers in Christ and fellow bishops, the members of our Holy Synod. This is in order that they may be better prepared, and when the time comes for necessary decisions to be made regarding this issue by the

Orthodox, Apostolic, and Autocephalous Church of Cyprus, they may decide correctly.

Before, however, I proceed to discuss the subject at hand, I feel the need to declare from the outset that I deeply respect and honor the venerable Ecumenical Patriarchate of Constantinople, that Great Church of Christ, not only because it has, according to the divine and sacred canons, the "place of honor"[12] and primacy among all the Orthodox Autocephalous Churches, but also for its unique and unparalleled contribution to the "One, Holy, Catholic and Apostolic Church."

No one can question the great contribution of the Ecumenical See of Constantinople to the unity of the universal Orthodox Church, in true faith, order, and love. The convocation, with the assistance of the respective emperor, of almost all the ecumenical councils, whether in Constantinople itself[13] or in cities under the ecclesiastical jurisdiction of the Ecumenical Patriarchate,[14] emphasized the exceptional ecclesiastical prestige of the see of the Queen of Cities.[15] It is also an indisputable fact that the church of Constantinople was illumined all the more by the exceptional prestige of the archbishops and patriarchs who, over the ages, occupied the ecumenical see (i.e., Gregory the Theologian, John Chrysostom, Nektarios, Proklos, Tarasios, Nikiforos, Fotios, and many others). The church of Constantinople was also made illustrious by the high spiritual level of her clergy, and by the dynamic witness of her monastic centers, such as the renowned Studion monastery, which made an enormous contribution to the ecclesiastical, spiritual, social, and cultural life of the Queen of Cities and of all Orthodoxy.

It would also be a serious omission if we neglected to emphasize the enormous capacity for missionary work that the Ecumenical Patriarchate of Constantinople has shown through the ages. Canon 28 of the Fourth Ecumenical Council defined the jurisdiction of the see of Constantinople not only "within the boundaries," but also "beyond the boundaries," which extended not only to the areas of Asia, Pontus, and Thrace, but also to the "barbarian lands," that is, beyond the administrative organism of the Byzantine Empire, thus outlining the future prospects of the missionary responsibility of the ecumenical see.

And indeed, "after the end of Iconoclasm, the missionary consciousness of the Ecumenical See was awakened in a remarkable manner, completely covering the vast area from Central Europe to the Volga and from the Balkans to the Baltic Sea with superbly-organized missions … " [16] "The whole of Central and Eastern Europe experienced the amazing spiritual mystagogy of the multifaceted cultural, religious, and social work of the Byzantine mission." [17]

Through this work, the new identity of the peoples of Eastern Europe was established and developed, and the Ecumenical Patriarchate emerged as the Mother Church of all these new local churches. Almost the entire rich cultural tradition of Byzantium was progressively transmitted to them. "All the nations, from Central Europe to the Caspian Sea and from the Balkans to the Baltic Sea, came to know the Christian faith from the missionary activity of the Ecumenical Patriarchate and came to live the experience of faith from the spiritual nourishment of the Mother Church." [18] We particularly respect and deeply honor the sacred memory of all the primates, archbishops, and patriarchs who, over the ages, adorned the ecumenical see of the Queen of Cities with their life and work.

The successive patriarchs of the ecumenical throne have always felt that the primacy which the see had been granted by the ecumenical councils was a "primacy of honor," not a "primacy of authority." They understood it as a "primacy of responsibility and ministry" for the unity of the Church in true faith and love. As primate of the leading see of the worldwide Orthodox Church, the ecumenical patriarch had, has and always will have, the canonical right:

a. Of honorary presidency of all the Orthodox Autocephalous Churches, as "first among equals" (*primus inter pares*);

b. Of coordinating the Orthodox churches in critical issues of inter-Orthodox interest;

c. Of expressing and implementing the decisions taken after a pan-Orthodox council or synaxis of the Orthodox primates;

d. Of granting autocephaly and autonomy, subject to the consent and approval of the other autocephalous Orthodox churches;

and finally,

e. The ecumenical patriarch, as primate of the leading see of the Orthodox Church, is the timeless guardian and guarantor, both of canonical order and of the authentic operation of the Orthodox, conciliar, democratic system.

Any misinterpretation or attempt to turn the above honorary prerogatives of the Ecumenical Patriarchate into a "primacy of authority" alters Orthodox ecclesiology, abolishes her conciliar, democratic system, and introduces a monarchical, papal-style authority, in which the ecumenical patriarch, transformed into a "Pope of the East," will speak *ex cathedra* for the Orthodox Church without the input of the other Orthodox primates. In such a situation, no bishop of the Orthodox Church can remain cold and indifferent. They must transform their passive anguish into active responsibility, stand up, and guided by their hierarchal conscience, fight, without fear or self-interest, against any unilateral act that interferes with the conciliarity of the Orthodox Church, threatening to divide ecumenical Orthodoxy.

Therefore, as a bishop in the Autocephalous Orthodox Church of the martyric island of the apostle Barnabas that is Cyprus, I feel a deep need to express my concerns, and to present my fears and anxieties regarding the current Ukrainian ecclesiastical issue, not only to the Christian plenitude of the Cypriot church, but also to the Orthodox Catholic Church of Christ in general. This problematic issue was created by Ecumenical Patriarch Bartholomew's recent unilateral decision to grant autocephaly to the church of Ukraine, and it has resulted in a difficult, divisive situation that is tormenting not only the Ukrainian Orthodox Church, but also worldwide Orthodoxy. It threatens the faith with the cursed crime of schism, an unforgivable and deadly sin, which, according to St John Chrysostom, " ... not even martyrdom of blood can wipe away."[19] That means that not even the blood of martyrdom, which is the most convincing proof of a passionate and living faith and trust in God, can wash away the deadly sin of schism.

Unfortunately, in our current difficult and wicked times, when the universal Orthodox Church of Christ should be united and strengthened in order to be in a position to give salvific answers to the contemporary challenges of our troubled times, it is with pain and sorrow that we see her vessel being tossed about by opposition and division amongst her leaders. This conflict, driven by egotism and lust for glory and power, frustratingly results in the Church being mocked and ridiculed by her enemies. In the face of Orthodoxy's current tragic situation, which reminds one of the horrific events of the Great Schism of 1054, and which threatens to rend the Lord's seamless garment for a second time, we hierarchs of the Orthodox Catholic Church of Christ do not have the right to remain cold and indifferent, immersed in our silence. We have an obligation to raise our voice and proclaim the truth boldly, without fear or passion, with the unaltered, secure protection of ecclesiastical tradition through the ages, hierocanonical order, and the Church's conciliar and hierarchical democratic system of governance, which is the guarantee of the preservation of ecclesiastical unity, and a basis for dealing with this crisis.

Doubtlessly, Ecumenical Patriarch Bartholomew's unilateral decision to grant autocephaly to a schismatic group of unrepentant, deposed, anathematized, and unordained pseudo-clergy, while ignoring the extant canonical Church in Ukraine under Metropolitan Onufry, creates an extremely serious ecclesiastical problem that threatens pan-Orthodox unity with a schism of enormous proportions. Therefore, we, as bishops of the Orthodox Church, who find ourselves in "the model and place of Christ," are obliged to raise a voice of protest. At the same time, without lethargic hesitation, as our hierarchal conscience dictates and the canonical tradition of the Orthodox Church demands and demonstrates, we must put forth ideas and recommendations in order to find a solution to this thorny Ukrainian issue, so that the salvific Orthodox unity which has been shaken may return. Otherwise, we will be complicit with those who, by their actions, are once more leading the Orthodox Church of Christ to a catastrophic schism.

The great twentieth-century thinker Georgios Theotokas wrote:

> A hierarch is not the head of a business, or a company, where it would be natural and fair for him to attach particular importance to his career, and his interests … The hierarch is a direct successor of the Apostles. He draws his authority from a mystical source and he expresses, with his very existence, the spirit of Christ. He is always prepared, as soon as he hears the bell that tolls the hour of sacrifice, to ascend to Calvary and be crucified for the good of mankind. And at that hour, he is overjoyed and gives thanks to God for choosing him.[20]

Today, when, under pressure from geopolitical, geostrategic and global economic interests, the Ukrainian issue threatens worldwide Orthodoxy with a catastrophic schism, all Orthodox bishops are called to reflect upon our responsibilities toward the Orthodox Church, as the critical circumstances of the present time require. The bell of duty is persistently tolling, and all hierarchs of the Orthodox Church of Christ ought to heed it. It is the greatest hubris is to accept the Church's internal upheavals passively and indifferently. A "fish-like silence"[21] is tantamount to guilt. Love for the Orthodox Church and her unity must kindle and magnify every bishop's inner flame, so that he may always be a responsible, ardent fighter for the unity of Orthodoxy.

Many canonists and distinguished academic theologians quite rightly emphasize that to better understand the so-called Ukrainian ecclesiastical issue, and whether or not His All-Holiness Patriarch Bartholomew rightly granted autocephaly, one must answer the three following questions:

a. Is the Church of Ukraine in the canonical jurisdiction of the Ecumenical Patriarchate of Constantinople, or the Patriarchate of Moscow?

b. Who is entitled to grant autocephaly, and under what conditions?

c. Does the Ecumenical Patriarchate have the prerogative of supreme canonical jurisdiction? That is, can it receive and arbitrate appeals beyond its jurisdictional borders from clergy of any rank who belong to any patriarchate and/or autocephalous church?

In addition to these three critical issues, a response to which is absolutely necessary for the proper understanding of the Ukrainian ecclesiastical question, the present work examines the following exceedingly important issues, which are the repercussions of the controversial Ukrainian question under discussion:

a. The interuption of Eucharistic communion between two Orthodox Churches.

b. Who is the head of the One, Holy, Catholic and Apostolic Church?

c. The tradition of the Great Endemic Synod of Constantinople.[22]

d. The conciliar and hierarchical system of governance of the worldwide Orthodox Church.

e. Conclusions.

f. Suggestions.

The entire study concludes with an epilogue, bibliography, and index.

To Which Patriarchate's Ecclesiastical Jurisdiction Does Ukraine Belong?

We must emphasize from the outset that it is universally acknowledged and undisputed that the Church of Russia, which until AD 1593 constituted a single unit with the Metropolis of Kiev, was under the canonical jurisdiction of the Ecumenical Patriarchate of Constantinople. According to historical sources, it was sixtieth in rank, and a metropolis of the Ecumenical Throne. In 1593, the four patriarchs of the East[23] elevated the church of Russia to a patriarchate, but the eparchy of Kiev continued to fall under the jurisdiction of the Patriarchate of Constantinople until 1686. During the seven centuries from 988 to 1686 (i.e., from the baptism of the Grand Prince of Kiev until the Patriarchal and Synodal Act of Patriarch Dionysius IV, in which the eparchy of Kiev was granted to the Russian Patriarchate), the Ecumenical Patriarchate fully exercised its canonical rights, primarily the two fundamental rights of ecclesiastical subordination. That is, the right to ordain and the right to judge bishops.

In 1686, however, the Metropolis of Kiev was united with the Russian Church. That same year, after Peter the Great annexed Ukraine to Russia, the then-patriarch of Constantinople, Dionysius IV, issued a patriarchal and synodal act declaring that "the Most Holy Eparchy of Kiev be subject to the Most Holy Patriarchal Throne of the great and God-fearing city of Muscovy."[24] Since then, the ancient patriarchates of Alexandria, Antioch, and Jerusalem, and subsequently all the other autocephalous Orthodox churches, have regarded the Ukrainian church as an integral part of the Patriarchate of Moscow, respecting Moscow's right to exercise ecclesiastical jurisdiction over the entire area of Ukraine.

Today, however, certain individuals within the leadership of the Ecumenical Patriarchate, Ecumenical Patriarch Bartholomew himself, his theological associates, and others, do not accept this reality, claiming that the Patriarchal and Synodical Act of 1686 did not cede the Metropolis of Kiev to the Patriarchate of Moscow completely and permanently, but rather *epitropikos* [in trust],[25] "that it may perpetually have"[26] only the right to ordain and enthrone the metropolitan of Kiev whom the clergy-laity assembly elects. They claim that this fact is documented in the mention of one of the terms included in the 1686 Letter of Issue, or Act, according to which the metropolitan of Kiev should, during the divine liturgy, commemorate the ecumenical patriarch first, "as his source and authority, and as superior to all dioceses and eparchies everywhere"[27] and then the current patriarch of Moscow. This reference to the decision in the 1686 Letter of Issue, namely, that the patriarch of Constantinople should be commemorated first, before the patriarch of Moscow, constitutes, they note, proof of the jurisdictional dependence of the Metropolis of Kiev on the Patriarchate of Constantinople. Therefore, they insist, on account of this term, the Metropolis of Kiev was never definitively and irrevocably ceded to the Patriarchate of Moscow.

The Orthodox Patriarchate of Moscow rejects these belated arguments from the Ecumenical Patriarchate, and points out that the text of the Patriarchal Act of 1686 does not mention any administrative authority that the Patriarchate of Constantinople retains over the ceded territory. Therefore, the wish expressed in the letter regarding the commemoration of the name of the patriarch of Constantinople first and the patriarch of Russia second has no connection to administrative responsibilities. They emphatically stress that it is not primarily the commemoration of a primate which determines a church's standing within a certain jurisdiction, but the right to ordain bishops (*jus ordinandi*) and the right to judge bishops (*jus jurandi*).

To support this argument, they refer to the distinguished professor of Church History at the University of Athens, and close associate and advisor of the Ecumenical Patriarchate, Vlasios Fidas. In less fractious times, Fidas wrote an article regarding the decree of the Third Ecumenical Council, which confirmed the autocephaly of the Church of Cyprus, noting the following: "It is clearly understood that the issue of the Church of Cyprus' administrative dependence on the jurisdiction of Antioch is inextricably linked to the canonical guarantee of its authority in the right to ordain and judge the metropolitan of Cyprus, since the fact that the Third Ecumenical Council did not cede this right to the bishop of Antioch preserved the autocephaly of the Church of Cyprus."[28]

Additionally, to avoid any misinterpretation, the Russian Church also refers to a surviving letter from Ecumenical Patriarch Dionysius IV to the czars of Russia, Ivan and Peter Alekseyevich, in which he explicitly states who has the right to administer the holy Metropolis of Kiev. In this letter to the czars of Muscovy, along with granting the patriarch of Moscow the right to consecrate the metropolitan of Kiev, he also grants him jurisdiction over the Metropolis of Kiev. In this letter, Patriarch Dionysius IV writes, among other things: "It is hereby granted that this holy Eparchy of Kiev be subject to the Most Holy Patriarchal Throne of the Holy and God-saved city of Muscovy … and they must recognize the Patriarch of Moscow as their elder and head, as they are consecrated by him … "[29]

These two texts, the Moscow Patriarchate stresses, make no reference to a temporary transfer of the Metropolis of Kiev, but on the contrary, emphasize the permanent and definitive character of its ecclesiastical subordination to the Russian Church.

In order for us to answer the question of whether the Church of Ukraine is subject to the Ecumenical Patriarchate of Constantinople or to the Patriarchate of Moscow, we must, in addition to the above, refer to the so-called *Syntagmatia* [Constitutions], which are widely acknowledged, not only by specialized canonists, but by all theologians, clergy and laity, academics and not, to constitute a true witness to the canonical jurisdiction of Orthodox patriarchates and autocephalous churches. Being listed in them is indisputable evidence as to where a diocese belongs. The mere listing of a metropolis in the

Syntagmatia of an autocephalous church, affirms, beyond any doubt, that this metropolis canonically belongs to that church.[30]

But what are these *Syntagmatia*, which, by common admission, have such great demonstrative power? A *Syntagmation*, according to Protopresbyter Anastasios Gotsopoulos, is the list of metropoles, archbishoprics and bishoprics, and their order of precedence within the framework of the ecclesiastical jurisdiction of the local Orthodox patriarchates and autocephalous churches. The *Syntagmatia* were formerly called *Taktika* (*Notitia Episcopatuum*), but today are published under various names, including *Imerologion, Diptycha, Epetiris, Typike Diataxis,* etc.[31]

We consider it appropriate to mention here that the oldest *taktikon* is the *Ekthesis of Epiphanius* from the early seventh century, according to which thirty-three metropoles, thirty-four archbishoprics and about 354 bishoprics were subject to the throne of Constantinople. "According to the *taktikon* of the Isaurian era (*Codex Parisinus Graecus 1555A*), in the mid-ninth century the Ecumenical Throne presided over 51 metropoles, 40 archbishoprics and approximately 608 bishoprics in its jurisdiction."[32] Turning, then, to the *Syntagmatia,* these indisputable witnesses of the canonical jurisdiction of the Patriarchal Thrones, we find that from AD 1686 onwards, no *Syntagmation* of any church lists the church of Ukraine as an eparchy of the Ecumenical Patriarchate. From the famous 1715 *Syntagmation* of the Patriarch Hrysanthos Notaras of Jerusalem in which Ukraine is listed as an eparchy of Muscovy and not the Ecumenical Patriarchate of Constantinople, until 2018, all the *Typika, Imerologia, Diptycha,* and *Epeterides* of all the autocephalous Orthodox churches everywhere consider Ukraine as part of the Russian Church. All the Orthodox churches recognized that the Church of Ukraine was subject to the canonical jurisdiction of Moscow, and considered Onufry to be the only canonical metropolitan of Kiev and All Ukraine.

Thus, for over 330 years, all the autocephalous Orthodox churches, without any exception, considered the Ukrainian Church to be under the ecclesiastical jurisdiction of the Patriarchate of Moscow, not the Ecumenical Patriarchate of Constantinople.

The fact that Ukraine was canonically transferred to the Patriarchate of Moscow by Ecumenical Patriarch Dionysius IV's 1686 Patriarchal Act, was also accepted by the Ecumenical Patriarchate itself, and is listed as such in the most official way in all its *Typika*, *Imerologia*, *Diptycha*, *Epeterides*, and *Typikas Diataxis* published by the patriarchal press in Constantinople. Some examples of this are the 1797 *Syntagmation* compiled by the ethnomartyr and hieromartyr Patriarch Gregorios V of Constantinople, as well as the *Syntagmatia* of 1829, 1896, and 1902, and all the *Syntagmatia* and *Epeterides* until 2018. In these official patriarchal publications, the Ecumenical Throne, without any reservation, accepted that Ukraine is canonically subject to the Patriarchate of Russia.

Additionally, Ecumenical Patriarch Bartholomew himself, in a speech to the Ukrainian people given on July 26, 2008, expressed the same ecclesiastical certainty (that Ukraine was ceded by the Ecumenical Patriarchate and now is subject to the Church of Russia). In that speech, the ecumenical patriarch stated:

The Ecumenical Patriarchate's sacrifice in the Orthodox Church, at the cost of its own rights, is even more clearly exemplified by the development of its relations with the eminent among the daughter Churches, the Church of Ukraine, which was under the Ecumenical Patriarchate's canonical jurisdiction for seven consecutive centuries, that is, from the baptism of the Grand Duchy of Kiev (988) until her annexation under Peter the Great (1687) to the Russian state. Indeed, for seven centuries the Mother Church offered "from her poverty".[33] Thus, after Ukraine's annexation to Russia, and under the pressure of Peter the Great, the Ecumenical Patriarch Dionysios IV judged that it was necessary in the circumstances of the time that the Church of Ukraine be ecclesiastically subject to the Patriarchate of Moscow.[34]

Moreover, in two letters of reply to the patriarch of Moscow, Ecumenical Patriarch Bartholomew recognized both the deposal (1992) and the anathematization (1997) that the Patriarchate of Moscow imposed on the former metropolitan of Kiev, Filaret. Responding to the first letter of Patriarch of Moscow Alexei of blessed memory regarding Filaret's deposal, Ecumenical Patriarch Bartholomew emphasized the following: "Our Holy Great Church of Christ recognizes the integral and exclusive jurisdiction of the Most Holy Church of Russia under your leadership regarding this issue, and accepts what has been synodically decided about the person in question, not desiring that the above cause any difficulty for our sister Church."[35]

In his second letter to the patriarch of Moscow (1997), he writes the following about the anathematization of Filaret: "Having received knowledge of the above decision, we will announce it to the Hierarchy of our Ecumenical throne and we will urge that henceforth they have no ecclesiastical communion with those mentioned."[36]

In other words, Ecumenical Patriarch Bartholomew recognized that the Patriarchate of Russia has not only the right to consecrate, but also the right to judge the bishops of Ukraine. That is to say, he recognizes the two fundamental rights of ecclesiastical jurisdiction: the right to ordain and the right to judge bishops. These two fundamental rights of ecclesiastical jurisdiction are also recognized by the Archbishop Ieronymos of Athens and All Greece, who later took the side of the Ecumenical Patriarchate as regards the Ukrainian Tome of Autocephaly. In his report to the Holy Synod of the Hierarchy of Greece, he noted the following: "We all know that the spread of the Gospel of salvation in Christ 'to all the nations' (Matthew 28:18–20) and 'to the ends of the earth' (Acts 1:7–8) made it necessary for the First Ecumenical Council to introduce the canonical institution of Autocephaly in all the Roman provinces of the Greco-Roman world for the synodal control of **the election, consecration and judgment of all the bishops of each province**"[37] (emphasis mine).

All these things, then, recommend and prove the full subordination of the Metropolis of Kiev to the canonical jurisdiction of the Patriarchate of Moscow, and, therefore, its non-dependence on the Ecumenical Patriarchate of Constantinople.

Parallel, however, to the indisputable testimony of the *Syntagmatia* and Patriarch Bartholomew's recognition of the canonical penalties of deposal and anathematization which the Patriarchate of Moscow imposed on the former metropolitan of Kiev, Filaret Denisenko, and by extension his recognition of the Patriarchate of Moscow's canonical jurisdiction over the Metropolis of Kiev, there are also studies by eminent historians and select members of the Ecumenical Patriarchate which were published in less fraught times and demonstrate that to which the *Syntagmatia* bear witness. That is, that for the past three and a half centuries, Kiev has not belonged to the canonical jurisdiction of the Patriarchate of Constantinople, but rather has been canonically subject to the Patriarchate of Moscow. Among these examples, we will mention:

(i) The archivist of the Ecumenical Patriarchate, who has deep knowledge of patriarchal documents, Archimandrite Kallinikos Delikanis. His famous three-volume work *Ecclesiastical Documents Preserved in the Codices of the Patriarchal Archive* published at the patriarchal press in Constantinople between 1902 and 1905, and reprinted by order of Ecumenical Patriarch Bartholomew in 1999, describes the Patriarchal and Synodal Act of Ecumenical Patriarch Dionysios IV as a "Synodal Tome" in which Patriarch Dositheos of Jerusalem also participated as a "fellow adjudicator." Delikanis also published the Synodal Letter of Ecumenical Patriarch Paisios to Patriarch Nikon of Moscow, in which the ecumenical patriarch calls the patriarch of Moscow "Patriarch of Moscow and Great and Little Russia."[38] As is well known, "Little Russia" is a name for Ukraine. Also, at another point in the work, the following is repeated: "The Metropolis of Kiev continued to be governed by representatives until its cession to the patriarchal throne of Moscow in 1686."[39]

(ii) Professor and Protopresbyter Theodoros Zisis (an old priest, associate, and advisor of the Ecumenical Patriarchate). When speaking at an international seminar of the Orthodox Center of the Ecumenical Patriarchate in Chambésy, Geneva, which took place in 1988, he stated that " … the Orthodox Russians of these countries, with Kiev at their center, continued, as a special metropolis, to be under the jurisdiction of the Ecumenical Patriarchate, even after the emancipation of Moscow from Constantinople, until 1686, when … Kiev was once more united to Moscow, and the union was restored with the approval of the Ecumenical Patriarchate."[40]

(iii) The professor of the University of Athens, Archimandrite Vasilios Stefanidis. In his book, *Ecclesiastical History from the Beginning until Today,* he notes the following interesting facts: "During the sixteenth century, Little Russia was politically united with Great Russia (1654), and after about thirty years it was also ecclesiastically united with it (1685). The union was ratified by the patriarch of Constantinople (1687) and thus all dependence of Little Russia on that patriarchate was so removed. The metropolitan of Kiev was under the jurisdiction of the patriarch of Moscow, who had been declared patriarch (since 1589)."[41]

(iv) The noted historian Metropolitan Varnavas D. Tzortzatos of Kitron. In his work *The Basic Institutions of Administration of the Orthodox Patriarchates with Historical Overviews* he notes: "During this new period of the Patriarchate of Moscow (1589–1700), in the context of basic administrative institutions, the notable ones were … and finally,

Ecumenical Patriarch Dionysios IV's administrative subordination of the Metropolis of Kiev, as well as missionary regions (Siberia, Iberia, Persia, etc.), to the Patriarchate of Moscow (1687)."[42]

(v) The Emeritus Professor of Ecclesiastical History, and one of the most important members of the Ecumenical Patriarchate, Vlasios Fidas, who long served as the dean of the Institute for Postgraduate Studies of Orthodox Theology of the Orthodox Center of the Ecumenical Patriarchate in Chambésy, Geneva, and was awarded the title and office of Master Teacher of the Church by the ecumenical patriarch. In one of his works, Professor Fidas notes, "Patriarch Dionysios of Constantinople ceded the Metropolis of Kiev to the canonical jurisdiction of the Patriarchate of Moscow (1687)."[43] In the same work, he emphasizes that Peter the Great abolished the patriarchal institution in Moscow and introduced a Synod. This decision was ratified by the ecumenical patriarch. Thus, the metropolitan of Kiev participates in the Synod of the Church of Russia as one of its three permanent members (alongside the metropolitans of Moscow and Saint Petersburg).[44]

Among other things, he emphatically notes that the Theological Academy of Kiev is one of the four most important academies of the Patriarchate of Moscow.[45] And again, in the same work, he also informs us that Metropolitan Vladimir of Kiev served as president of the Pan-Russian Council of 1917, in which the patriarchal see was restored in Russia.[46] Finally, in the same book, the *Ecclesiastical History of Russia*, the very respected and renowned Professor Fidas refers to the particularly important Council of 1945, which took place with inter-Orthodox participation, and drafted, as he informs us, the Rules of Procedure of the Orthodox Church of Russia. He emphatically states that according to Article 19 of the Rules, the metropolitan of Kiev participates as a permanent member in the six-member Permanent Synod.[47]

Indeed, it raises the question of why this renowned and eminent university professor of Ecclesiastical History and favored theological associate of Ecumenical Patriarch Bartholomew, the very dear and respected Vlasios Fidas, denies his own scientific publications and conclusions, which clarified the Patriarchate of Moscow's full and canonical jurisdiction over Ukraine.

If one reads his latest study on the Synodal Act of 1686 and the Autocephaly of the Ukrainian Church, one will be left speechless by his novel, contradictory assertions, by which, in his effort to support the actions of His All-Holiness Patriarch Bartholomew, he undoes his own previous writing.[48]

It would, however, be an omission if we did not mention the famous theologian of the Orthodox Church and reverend hierarch of the Ecumenical Throne, His Eminence Metropolitan Kallistos Ware of Diokleia who, in an interview in December, 2018, also mentioned the ecclesiastical situation in Ukraine, and pointed out the reasons for which he did not support the Phanar's decision. According to His Eminence, the restoration of the Ukrainian schismatics was an enormous mistake by Patriarch Bartholomew. "Though I am a metropolitan of the Ecumenical Patriarchate," he said, "I am not at all happy about the position taken by Patriarch

Bartholomew. With all due respect to my Patriarch, I am bound to say that I agree with the view expressed by the Patriarchate of Moscow that Ukraine belongs to the Russian Church."[49]

At another point, His Eminence states, "After all, the Metropolis of Kiev by the agreement of 1676 [sic] was transferred from the omophorion of the Ecumenical Patriarchate to that of the Patriarchate of Moscow. So, for 330 years Ukraine has been part of the Russian Church."[50] In this same interview, this eminent theologian and metropolitan of the Ecumenical Throne also noted that "I feel that it was unwise of the Patriarch of Constantinople unilaterally to say the agreement of 1676 [sic] is cancelled. After all, as Aristotle says, even God cannot change the past."[51]

In addition to all the historical evidence that we have cited above, it is incumbent on us to submit the following two further references, which bear witness to the fact that the Ukrainian Church belongs to the Orthodox Patriarchate of Moscow:

(1) "When, in the remote year of 1869, the Russian Orthodox Church sent a written reply to the Patriarchate of Constantinople regarding the ecclesiastical issue in Bulgaria, at the end of the letter, alongside the signatures of the Metropolitans of Moscow and St. Petersburg, there was the signature of Metropolitan Arseny of Kiev and Galicia (in second place!), the Church of Constantinople did not react. This happened again in another letter in 1871."

ii) "When in 1976 the then Metropolitan Filaret Denisenko of Kiev and Galicia led a delegation of the Russian Orthodox Church at the pre-conciliar conference in Geneva, the patriarchate of Constantinople again did not protest."[52]

It is necessary, however at this point to indicate the following very important fact: even if it were proven that the Ukrainian Church is, according to the sacred canons, under the Ecumenical Patriarchate of Constantinople, and, therefore, for the past 330 years or more its jurisdictional rights were violated by the Autocephalous Church of the Patriarchate of Moscow, then the Ecumenical Patriarchate of Constantinople should have attempted to exercise its jurisdictional rights within the period of time determined by the sacred canons, and, if prevented from doing this, should have expressed its justified protest. In the canonical tradition of the Orthodox Church there are clearly defined timeframes within which a protest over a violation of jurisdictional rights is permitted. After the deadline, the Church whose jurisdictional rights are being violated is no longer allowed to appeal to the appropriate ecclesiastical bodies in order to resolve the dispute and restore its right. According to the sacred canons, there is a prescribed period of time during which legal differences between two churches can be resolved. After this period of time, the bishop who has allegedly been wronged can no longer make claims.

According to the holy seventeenth canon of the Fourth Ecumenical Council, and canon 25 of the Sixth Ecumenical Council, the limit of time for jurisdictional disputes is thirty years.

Canon 17 of the Fourth Ecumenical Council states:

Outlying or rural parishes in every province will remain subject to the bishops who now have jurisdiction over them, particularly if these bishops have continuously governed them without coercion for thirty years. But if within the thirty years there has been, or is, any dispute concerning them, it is lawful for those who hold themselves aggrieved to bring their cause before the synod of the province. But if anyone has been wronged by his metropolitan, let the matter be decided by the exarch of the diocese or by the throne of Constantinople, as aforesaid.[53]

Canon 25 of the Sixth Ecumenical Council states: "Additionally, we renew the canon which orders that country parishes, and those which are in the provinces, remain subject to the bishops over them; especially if for thirty years they had administered them without opposition. But if within thirty years there had been or should be any controversy on the point, it is lawful for those who think themselves injured to refer the matter to the provincial synod."[54]

I firmly believe that given all the historical and canonical facts we have just referenced, the first question has been fully answered. That is, "To whose ecclesiastical jurisdiction does the Orthodox Church of Ukraine belong?" All the historical and canonical facts which we have quoted recommend and prove the full subordination of the Metropolis of Ukraine to the canonical jurisdiction of the Patriarchate of Moscow, and, consequently, its non-dependence on the Ecumenical Patriarchate of Constantinople. For this very reason, the unilateral rejection of the validity of the 1686 *Letter*, the Patriarchate of Constantinople's anticanonical appropriation of jurisdictional rights over the territories of Ukraine, and the grant of autocephaly to Ukraine constitute an act of incursion into another's canonical territory. They are in direct opposition to the sacred canons of the Orthodox Church, which do not permit the violation of jurisdictional boundaries and the simultaneous existence of multiple jurisdictions in the same locale. According to the sacred canons, the unilateral and arbitrary intervention of a local autocephalous church in the internal affairs of another constitutes an irregular act and a canonical offense which is condemned by many holy canons. Some examples of this are Canon 2 of the Second Ecumenical Council and Canon 8 of the Third Ecumenical Council. Canon 2 of the Second Ecumenical Council states that "Bishops are not to go beyond their own dioceses to churches lying outside of their boundaries, nor bring confusion to the churches, but let the Bishop of Alexandria, according to the canons, alone administer the affairs of Egypt, and let the bishops of the East manage the affairs of the East without intervention, the privileges of the Church of Antioch, which are mentioned in the canons of Nicaea, being preserved."[55]

The decree of the fathers of the Third Ecumenical Council of Ephesus, by which they strictly forbid the intervention of a primate of an autocephalous church into the affairs of another, is also noteworthy. This Canon reads as follows:

> None of the Bishops, beloved of God, will assume control of any province which has not heretofore, from the very beginning, been under their own jurisdiction, or that of his predecessors. But if anyone has violently taken and subjected a province, he shall give it up lest the Canons of the Fathers be transgressed or the vanities of worldly honor be brought in under pretext of sacred office; or we lose, without our knowledge, little by little, the liberty which Our Lord Jesus Christ, the Deliverer of all, has given us by His Own Blood. Wherefore, this holy and ecumenical Synod has decreed that in every province the rights which heretofore, from the beginning, have belonged to it, shall be preserved to it ...

And if any one shall bring forward a rule contrary to what is here determined, this holy and ecumenical Synod unanimously decrees that it shall be of no effect.[56]

In this chapter we have ascertained, as I have already pointed out, that there has been a violation of the holy canons, or if you prefer, a selective, contradictory, self-serving interpretation of them. Therefore, the passage in Canon 8 of the Third Ecumenical Council, "lest the Canons of the Fathers be transgressed" is very interesting and should not be left unaddressed. The same insistence on the strict observance of the holy canons is also emphasized by Canon 1 of the Fourth Ecumenical Council, which states: "We have deemed it just that the canons set forth by the holy Fathers at each council until now remain in force."[57] This canon stipulates that all the holy canons issued by the Holy Fathers at each previous Ecumenical Council are valid, and are to remain unchanged and enforced. Indeed, Canon 2 of the Sixth Ecumenical Council in Trullo also warns, "No one is to transgress or disregard the aforesaid canons, or to receive others beside them, falsely set forth by individuals who have attempted to barter with and sell the truth. And if anyone is convicted of innovating on, or attempting to overturn, any of the aforementioned canons, he will be subject to the penalty which that canon imposes, and so by it to be cured of his transgression."[58]

In addition to these Canons, the first canon of the Seventh Ecumenical Council also strictly commands:

We gladly embrace the divine canons, holding fast all the precepts of the same, complete and unchanged, whether they have been set forth by the holy trumpets of the Spirit, the renowned Apostles, or by the Six Ecumenical Councils, or by local Councils assembled to promulgating the decrees of the said Ecumenical Councils, or by our holy Fathers. For all these, being illumined by the same Spirit, defined such things as were expedient. Accordingly, those whom they placed under anathema, we likewise anathematize; those whom they deposed, we also depose; those whom they excommunicated, we also excommunicate; and those whom they delivered over to punishment, we subject to the same penalty.[59]

The Holy Fathers who comprised the respective Ecumenical Councils demand the faithful and strict observance of the holy canons, and absolutely no one should, for any reason or under any pretext, violate them, or even interpret them differently at different times, according to one's current preferences. It is well known that the word *nomimon* [legal] is a palindrome, so it can be read in either direction. The metaphorical meaning of this lexical phenomenon can be observed in the legal practice, where a certain law can elicit diametrically opposing interpretations, depending on people's expectations and desires. I am sorry to say that unfortunately this can be observed in the events which we are analyzing, and which move me, on account of the prevarications that I observe, to think of the story, deep in our collective memory, of Nasreddin Hodja's oven, which turns according to people's moods [Nasreddin Hodja is a character in jokes and folktales throughout the Arabic-speaking world, and by extension countries which were in contact with them. In the story referenced here, Hodja decides to build an oven. A series of neighbors visit, each suggesting he build the oven door in a different direction, all for a different reason. Finally, he decides to build his oven on a cart so he can turn it around according to the wishes of each]. The sacred canons are landmarks which were instituted and interpreted, through the Holy Spirit, by our Holy Fathers in council, and with which we should comply if we want good order in the Church. The peaceful operation of the conciliar, hierarchical, and democratic system of governance which characterizes and regulates the Orthodox Church, depends on whether or not the sacred Canons are faithfully observed.

The late professor of Canon Law, Amilkas Alivizatos, wrote the following in his *Introduction to the Collection of the Holy Canons*: " ... praying that the proper, faithful, and strict implementation of the provisions of the canons and ecclesiastical laws may secure the stability of ecclesiastical life, and may ensure that the Church is shown to be the primary agent of true social restoration in the spirit of Christ."[60]

This was not by chance. In the same introduction, this distinguished professor adds the following: "The decisions of the Ecumenical Councils, whether in regards to dogmatic issues, put forth in the 'Terms', administrative matters adjudicated in the canons, or juridical decisions that were definitively and finally issued ... are absolutely mandatory for each individual Orthodox Church. In dogmatic matters, they are immutable and unerring. In administrative and juridical matters, they are irrevocable, and any modification to them is only possible through the decision of a new Ecumenical Council."[61]

"This Greek professor's views," notes Protopresbyter Professor Dimitrios Konstantelos, "are corroborated by canonists of other Orthodox Churches. We will limit ourselves to one more witness. The Russian professor of Canon Law, Nikolai Afanasiev. Although at first glance he presents certain contradictions in his opinions, he writes that 'canonical decrees, like dogmatic decrees, are divinely-inspired, though they should not be seen in the same light … Dogma is the absolute truth and the Canons are the practical application and expression of these truths.' According to these views, both dogmas and the Canons are made absolute."[62]

In conclusion, we again emphatically state that the faithful and strict application of the sacred Canons is imperative because contemptuous violation of them does not bring ease, peace, and unity, but rather anomaly, turmoil, and discord within the Church.

The Right to and Conditions under Which Autocephaly May Be Granted

I believe that the most convincing answer to the question of who has the right to grant autocephaly to a local church and under what conditions is given by Ecumenical Patriarch Bartholomew himself. According to the position he expressed in an interview he gave in January, 2001 to the Greek newspaper *Nea Ellada* [New Greece]: "Autocephaly and autonomy are granted by the whole church through a decision of the Ecumenical Council. Since, for various reasons, convening an Ecumenical Council is not possible, the Ecumenical Patriarchate, as the coordinator of all the Orthodox Churches, grants autocephaly or autonomy, provided that they (the other Orthodox Churches) give their approval."[63]

Ecumenical Patriarch Athenagoras, of blessed memory, expresses the same position in his July 27, 1961, letter to the then patriarch of Bulgaria, Kirill. He writes: " … in the certain conviction and expectation that this decision regarding the following events will have the approval and consent of their Eminences, the most reverend Patriarchs and Primates of the other Autocephalous Orthodox Churches."[64]

This truth, that the granting of autocephaly requires pan-Orthodox consent, is also confirmed by Patriarch

Bartholomew's closest collaborator and advisor, John Zizioulas, Metropolitan of Pergamos. Serving as president of the inter-Orthodox Preparatory Conference in Geneva on December 9–17, 2009, Zizioulas stressed the following crucial facts:

> If the Ecumenical Patriarch secures the consent of the local Autocephalous Orthodox Churches by obtaining their written consent, he may sign the Patriarchal Tome on his own … if the Ecumenical Patriarch alone signs the Tome of Autocephaly, pan-Orthodox consensus is in no way degraded, as he is acting on what has already been decided. The consent of all the Primates and naturally, also the Primate of the Mother Church, should have been given in advance. The Ecumenical Patriarchate has a coordinating ministry, and can express the opinion of all Orthodoxy. And he does this after having communicated with all the other Primates. This has no relation to papal primacy. The Pope expresses his opinion without asking others. The Ecumenical Patriarch seeks to secure the opinion of others and then simply expresses it.[65]

Distinguished university professors also attest to the above. As an indication, we will mention just two of them, Vlasios Fidas and Vasilios Stavridis. In his work published in 1979, Professor Fidas states that "An Ecumenical Council, or the unanimous agreement of all the Patriarchal Thrones, constitutes the canonical mechanism for proclaiming a Church autocephalous or autonomous. Any other procedure is anti-canonical and not only does not serve unity, but completely to the contrary. By violating canonical tradition, it erodes and fractures the unity of the Church in correct faith and love."[66]

Likewise, Professor Vasilios Stavridis, in a special study on the history of the Ecumenical Patriarchate, states the following: "The Ecumenical Patriarch has certain rights ... granting and recognizing the autocephaly or elevation to patriarchal see in ecclesiastical regions that were previously under him, having met the canonical conditions for it, in accordance with the unanimous opinion of the other sister Orthodox Churches."[67]

Therefore, based on the above, without hesitation or vacillation, we once more stress the following: the Ecumenical Patriarchate of Constantinople has, according to the divine and holy canons (Canon 3 of the Third Ecumenical Council and Canon 28 of the Fourth Ecumenical Council), "privileges of honor" among all the Patriarchal Thrones of the East. After the Great Schism of 1054, the Ecumenical Patriarchate happens to be first in honor in the One, Holy, Catholic and Apostolic Church, and has the canonical right of the honorary Presidency of the Autocephalous Orthodox Churches. The ecumenical patriarch, as "first among equals" (*primus inter pares*), has the right to preside in the case of an Ecumenical Council, and also the task of coordinating the Orthodox Churches. He is entitled to grant autocephaly or autonomy in an ecclesiastical province, but under certain clear and strict conditions, which have been established by ecclesiastical tradition and are consistent with Orthodox ecclesiology and canonical order. Moreover, these conditions are the same as those that were agreed upon by the representatives of all the local Orthodox Churches at the 1993 and 2009 meetings of the inter-Orthodox Preparatory Commission for the Great and Holy Council of Crete (2016).[68]

This joint decision of the autocephalous Orthodox Churches, regarding accepting the procedure for granting autocephaly made at the pre-conciliar conferences for the preparation of the Great and Holy Council, was written down in "Autocephaly and the Manner of Proclaiming It," which was signed by the representatives of all the Orthodox Churches and is entirely in accordance with Orthodox ecclesiology and canonical order. It provides for the following:

(a) A request for autocephaly made by an ecclesiastical body;

(b) Consent from the Mother Church from which the ecclesiastical province requesting autocephaly is being detached;

(c) Approval from all the other autocephalous Orthodox Churches.

Unfortunately, the text of this joint decision was never presented at the Great and Holy Council in Kolymbari in Crete. Some claim that this was due to the Russian Church's disagreement regarding the manner in which a Tome of Autocephaly should be signed. Following its session on October 17, 2019, however, the Holy Synod of the Church of Russia released an official statement informing the public that "Actually, the topic of autocephaly was excluded from the agenda of the Council much earlier, after Patriarch Bartholomew's consistent pleas to do so."[69]

So, the first thing that a church desiring autocephaly must do, is express through her Christian *pleroma* (clergy and laity) her desire for autocephaly. She must then submit this desire, as a request, to the Ecumenical Patriarchate for examination.

At this point it must be especially emphasized that the request for autocephaly should be made by the entirety of the Christian *pleroma,* or, at the very least, by the vast majority, not by a small minority, and not by uncanonical, schismatic groups.

After this, the ecumenical patriarch should inquire with the Mother Church (the Church from which the Ecclesiastical Province making the request will be detached) to see if she gives her consent. After securing the Mother Church's agreement, the Ecumenical Patriarchate should relay the request for autocephaly to the other Orthodox Churches, so there can be pan-Orthodox consensus. As the coordinating center of Orthodoxy, the Ecumenical Patriarchate should initiate consultations with all the other autocephalous Orthodox churches in order to ensure they all agree to the granting of autocephaly.

Regarding Ukraine, with which we are currently concerned, we highlight the following: the Ecumenical Patriarchate would only be able to receive and consider a request for autocephaly from an ecclesiastical organization which meets the canonical requirements. However, as we all know, the only canonical ecclesiastical structure in Ukraine is the one under Metropolitan Onufry, which is recognized by all the Orthodox Churches, and until recently even by the Ecumenical Patriarchate. It is the autonomous Church of Ukraine, and its 90 bishops, 12,500 parishes, 250 monasteries, 5,000 monks and nuns, and tens of millions of faithful, which constitutes the vast majority of the Ukrainian Orthodox people.

However, this canonical, autonomous Church, which since 1686 has been under the ecclesiastical jurisdiction of the

Patriarchate of Moscow, did not seek, as it has every right to do, nor has it ever accepted, autocephaly from anyone.

The autocephaly of the Ukrainian Orthodox Church was pursued, requested, and received by, two schismatic groups:

a) The "Kievan Patriarchate of the Ukrainian Orthodox Church," which anticanonically seceded from the Russian Patriarchate, and which is headed by the deposed and anathematized former metropolitan of Kiev, the monk Filaret Denisenko, and

b) The "Ukrainian Autocephalous Orthodox Church," led by the unordained Makary Maletich, "deposed former priest of the Russian Church 'consecrated' as a pseudo-bishop by a deposed Bishop and the deposed deacon of the Russian Church, Victor-Vitaly-Victor Chekalin, a tragic personality with a rich 'history' as an 'Orthodox' pseudo-bishop, Uniate, Protestant Pastor, and convicted pedophile who was given retirement, being declared legally insane in Australia."[70]

Makary Maletich, not having any canonical episcopal consecration, and yet proclaiming himself "Metropolitan of Kiev and All Ukraine," is the one who led the renaissance of Vasyl Lypkivsky's 1921 "Movement," which, in 1980, was revived by the self-proclaimed "patriarch" Mstislav, who lived in the West. It should, therefore, be noted, that as someone who is essentially unordained and devoid of apostolic succession, Makary Maletich most likely traces the origin of his consecration to a "bishop" from Vasyl Lypkivsky's Movement.

[This movement was created in 1921 by the Soviet authorities, who wished to cause division in the Orthodox Church of Ukraine and weaken the position of the Russian Church and

Patriarch Tikhon. The pseudo-bishop Vasyl Lypkivsky rejected the holy canons of the Seven Ecumenical Councils, adopting his own, new, so-called Kievan Canons and established a married hierarchy without apostolic succession, after adopting the theory of the ideological leader of the "Brotherhood of the Workers of the Word," Vladimir Chekovsky. According to Chekovsky, it is not the bishops who have the grace of the Holy Spirit, but the Church, that is, the community of the faithful. This community of the faithful is therefore able, on its own, and without the participation of bishops, to ordain a candidate for holy orders and grant him the grace and gifts of the Holy Spirit. Vasyl Lypkivsky was consecrated to the episcopate in this exact way, not by bishops, but by presbyters, hierodeacons, and laypeople. "The oldest man having first read the prayers of ordination, all the members of the assembly placed their hands on each other's shoulders, those in the solea on the shoulders of the deacons, the deacons on the priests, and the priests on the candidate for consecration. With ecclesiastical hymns and prayers, they vested the candidate in a bishop's stole ... "[71]]

It is truly impossible to understand how Ecumenical Patriarch Bartholomew, contrary to what he had previously declared in less fractious times, could, on his own, without the prior approval and consent of the other autocephalous Orthodox Churches, and particularly the Mother Church of Russia, from which the Church of Ukraine would be detached, grant autocephaly, not to the canonical Church under Metropolitan Onufry, but to two schismatic groups (that of the deposed Filaret and that of Makary, who was unordained and lacking apostolic succession).

After restoring this conglomeration of deposed, anathematized, self-consecrated, and unrepentant schismatics to canonical order with a patriarchal Act, the venerable Ecumenical Patriarchate proceeded to hold a so-called Unifying Council, which elected "Metropolitan" Epiphany Dumenko, who was "ordained" by the deposed and anathematized Filaret Denisenko, as primate, and granted the new "church" resulting from these actions "Autocephaly," as the "Orthodox Church in Ukraine." All this, while the canonical Orthodox Church under Metropolitan Onufry of Kiev and All Ukraine, which unites the vast majority of Orthodox Christians in Ukraine, is despised and persecuted.

One is truly aghast in the face of all these recent ecclesiologically unacceptable and anticanonical events that have taken place in the Orthodox Church of Ukraine. Can the ecumenical patriarch, on his own, sign a unilateral act nullifying the deposal of canonically deposed individuals whose deposal was recognized at a pan-Orthodox level? Can he remedy the lack of apostolic succession of self-consecrated individuals, and subsequently grant these unrepentant schismatic groups a Tome of Autocephaly?

We all know that in the Eastern Orthodox Church we do not have a papal system, according to which the pope decides (*definimus*) and everyone else obeys. In the Orthodox Church we have the conciliar democratic system, according to which all the autocephalous Churches, under the presidency of the Ecumenical Patriarchate of Constantinople, gather synodically and decide how to treat schisms and apply appropriate *economia* (spiritual leniency) to invalid consecrations. This is why during Epiphany's "enthronement," no primate (apart from the ecumenical patriarch), or bishop of another Autocephalous Church was in attendance, and none of their representatives sent the customary congratulatory letter. Moreover, for an entire year, no Orthodox Church recognized the pseudo-autocephaly which had been granted to that marginal group of schismatics. This period of non-recognition is something unprecedented in ecclesiastical history. Even today, all the churches, with the exception of the Patriarchate of Alexandria and the Church of Greece, which, for their own reasons, accepted the Tome after a year, continue to resist and to refuse to recognize Epiphany.

As is to be expected, this abuse of the sacred institution of autocephaly not only did not lead to the desired peace and unity, but, on the contrary, brought even greater turmoil and division to the life of the Ukrainian people, who have been through so many trials and tribulations already, and created a deep crisis both in the Ukrainian Orthodox Church and in Orthodoxy worldwide.

In Ukraine today there is the canonical metropolitan of Kiev and All Ukraine, Onufry, Epiphany, the so-called primate of the "Orthodox Autocephalous Church of Ukraine," and, Filaret, who was granted the title of "Honorary Patriarch" by the so-called Unifying Council, but who then withdrew his original agreement, and does not accept the Tome of Autocephaly, as it abolished the "Patriarchate" which he himself had previously proclaimed.

Some hierarchs in Greece claim that Ecumenical Patriarch Bartholomew would not have proceeded with granting autocephaly to the Church of Ukraine if the Orthodox Patriarchate of Russia had not declined the invitation to, and had not been absent from, the Council of Crete (2016). They believe that as the issue of autocephaly concerned them, it would have been discussed, a solution would have been found, and there would not now be any issue.

However, is it possible for any reasonable person to justify the unorthodox, anticanonical, unilateral, and self-willed grant of autocephaly as retaliation for the Patriarchate of Moscow not attending the Great and Holy Council in Crete? It is not possible for autocephaly to be used as a disciplinary measure or punishment for disobedience, as the contemptuous violation of the holy canons does not bring good order, peace, and unity, but rather anomaly, turmoil, and discord in the heart of the Church.

Thus, to be brief, we will state that none of the three basic conditions for granting autocephaly were met in the case of Ukraine, because:

i) The granting of autocephaly was not requested by the universally acknowledged Church of Ukraine under Metropolitan Onufry, but rather by two much smaller schismatic groups.

ii) The role of the Mother Church, in this case the Orthodox Church of Russia, was contemptuously and completely disregarded.

iii) Ecumenical Patriarch Bartholomew proceeded to grant autocephaly without any contact or consultation with the primates of the other Autocephalous Orthodox Churches.

Does the Ecumenical Patriarchate Have the Canonical Right to Receive Appeals from Appellants beyond Its Jurisdictional Borders?

This issue, whether or not the Ecumenical Patriarchate has the canonical right to receive appeals across jurisdictional boundaries from clergy of any rank, not only from within its own jurisdiction, but also from the jurisdiction of the other Patriarchal Thrones and Autocephalous Churches, occupied the whole of the Orthodox Church following the Council of Sardica (present-day Sofia) in 343. It was on the basis of the canons of this council that the bishop of Rome asserted that he had the right and privilege to receive the appeals of bishops and clergy not only from his own canonical jurisdiction, but also from other Churches.

The Ecumenical Patriarchate of Constantinople invokes Sardican canons 3, 4, and 5 to support the argument that it has the responsibility and canonical right to receive and pronounce judgment on appeals from clergy from all the local Autocephalous Orthodox Churches, since, it states, the Fourth Ecumenical Council of Chalcedon granted the bishop of New Rome (Constantinople) the same privileges as the bishop of Old Rome.

It is a true and undeniable fact that the Fourth Ecumenical Council of Chalcedon (451) instituted Canon 28 which, as mentioned earlier, grants the bishop of Constantinople the same privileges as the primate of the Church of Rome. This canon is as follows:

> We also do enact and decree the same things concerning the privileges of the most holy Church of Constantinople, which is New Rome. For the Fathers rightly granted privileges to the throne of old Rome, because it was the royal city. And the One Hundred and Fifty Bishops, beloved of God, (*sic*, it was 650 bishops) moved by the same consideration, gave equal privileges to the most holy throne of New Rome, justly judging that the city which is honored with the Sovereignty and the Senate, and enjoys equal privileges with the old imperial Rome, should in ecclesiastical matters also be magnified as she is, and rank second to her.[72]

Therefore, if the Orthodox bishop of Old Rome had the privilege of supreme ecclesiastical jurisdiction, and consequently the right to receive appeals from clergy of Churches other than the ones under his ecclesiastical jurisdiction, then this would also apply to the ecumenical patriarch of Constantinople. If, however, the bishop of Rome did not have supreme ecclesiastical jurisdiction, then the ecumenical patriarch of Constantinople does not have it either, since the text of Canon 28 of the Fourth Ecumenical Council is categorical. The patriarch of Constantinople is granted the same rights, neither more nor less, than those of Rome.

Canons 36 and 134 of the Council of Carthage (Canons 31 and 129 according to the numbering of the *Rudder*) give us the key to the meaning and application of Canons 3, 4, and 5 of the Council of Sardica. These canons refer only to Rome's privilege of receiving appeals from clergy and bishops of her own jurisdiction, not from clergy of other churches.

The great and significant Council of Carthage was convened in 418, and, among other issues, dealt diligently with the problem of Apiarius, a priest belonging to the bishopric of Sicca in Africa. The council lasted for six years, from 418 to 424, and over the course of this period three consecutive popes presided over the Patriarchate of Rome: Zosimus, Boniface, and Celestine. The Council of Carthage established 124 canons and issued two letters, one to Zosimus and Boniface, and one to Celestine. The canons and letters were confirmed specifically and definitively by Canon 2 of the Holy Sixth Ecumenical Council, and so received pan-Orthodox standing. The issue of Apiarius began as follows: Zosimus, bishop of Rome, erroneously citing the canons of Sardica as "canons of the First Ecumenical Council," claimed to be able to adjudicate appeals from bishops and other clergy of the Churches of North Africa.

By his own counsel, and basing his decision on Canon 5 of the Council of Sardica, Zosimus agreed to hear the appeal of Apiarius (a priest from the Church of Carthage who was convicted of canonical offenses and deposed). He sent representatives to Carthage, insisting that they reexamine Apiarius's case and notify him of its progress, so he could make a final decision himself. The African bishops unequivocally denied the bishop of Old Rome's claimed right to act as supreme arbiter in their churches, and they strictly forbade their clergy from making appeals "across the sea," that is, to Rome. They then sent a letter to Zosimus's successor, Pope

Boniface, in which they rebutted Zosimus's erroneous claims in calling the canons of Sardica "canons of the First Ecumenical Council." This rebuttal was based on the document of the acts of the First Ecumenical Council of Nicaea, which were preserved in the Churches of the East. The 217 bishops present at the Council of Carthage then asked Pope Boniface: "Who can doubt that the copies of the Nicene Council gathered in the Greek empire are most accurate, which although brought together from so diverse and from such noble Greek churches are found to agree when compared together?"[73]

In 423, however, Apiarius once more appealed to Zosimus and Boniface's successor, Pope Celestine, who also sent his legates to Carthage, insisting on Apiarius's acquittal. The Council gathered once more in Carthage in 424 to address the pope of Rome's purported right to receive appeals from bishops and clergy outside his own jurisdiction, and again rejected it. They sent a second letter, this time to Pope Celestine, rebuking him, and stating that no one would wish to believe that God would have given all proper judgment to one bishop alone (of Rome), and not to so many bishops gathered in council: "Who is it who will believe that our God can inspire any single person with righteous justice while refusing it to countless bishops gathered in a council?"[74] In another place in the letter, the Council asks Pope Celestine: "Moreover if anyone asks you to send any of your clergy here to adjudicate their appeal, do not comply, lest it seem that we are introducing the pride of secular dominion into the Church of Christ which shows the light of simplicity and the dawn of humility to all that desire to see God."[75] And again, "Do not readily receive those coming from here and from now on do not desire to receive into communion those who have been excommunicated by us."[76]

According to the above, the claim of the then-Orthodox bishop of Old Rome to a privilege of supreme ecclesiastical jurisdiction was rejected by the Church. The Holy Sixth Ecumenical Council accepted the canonical decree of the Council of Carthage, which stated that clergy of an ecclesiastical jurisdiction outside the bounds of the Roman Patriarchate who appeal their cases to the bishop of Old Rome are excommunicated. Canon 36 (31 according to the numbering of the *Rudder*) of the Council of Carthage states the following:

> If priests, deacons, or other members of the lower clergy have an issue, and are dissatisfied with the judgment of their own bishop, let the neighboring bishops, with the consent of their own bishop, hear them out, and let the bishops who have been called in judge between them. But if they think they have cause for appeal from the judgment of the neighboring bishops, they shall not betake to ask for adjudication from beyond the seas, but from the primates of their own provinces, or else to a universal council, as has also been decreed concerning bishops. But whoever thinks it proper to carry an appeal across the water will not be received into communion by anyone within the boundaries of Africa.[77]

Canon 34 of the same council, which is almost indistinguishable from Canon 36 (129 and 31, respectively, according to the numbering of the *Rudder*), states:

> It seemed good that presbyters, deacons, or other of the lower clergy who are to be tried, if they question the decision of their bishops, the neighboring bishops having been invited by them

with the consent of their bishops, shall hear them and determine whatever separates them. But should they think an appeal should be carried from them, let them not carry the appeal except to African councils or to the primates of their provinces. But whoever shall think of carrying an appeal across seas he shall be admitted to communion by no one in Africa.[78]

The undivided church therefore recognized that Canons 3, 4, and 5 of the Council of Sardica concerned the special privilege granted to the Orthodox bishop of Old Rome only in regard to bishops and clergy within his own jurisdiction. It did not grant Old Rome supreme ecclesiastical jurisdiction, and therefore the same applies to the bishop of New Rome, the ecumenical patriarch of Constantinople. Thus, he also has the special privilege of receiving appeals, but only from bishops and clergy from churches subject to him, namely, the churches of Thrace, Pontus, and Asia, as Canon 28 of the Fourth Ecumenical Council decrees. "Only the metropolitans of the Pontic, Asian and Thracian Dioceses ... should be consecrated by the aforementioned most holy throne of the most holy Church in Constantinople."[79]

In addition to the way it interprets Canons 3, 4, and 5 of the Council of Sardica, the Ecumenical Patriarchate of Constantinople also refers to Canons 9 and 17 of the Fourth Ecumenical Council in Chalcedon, claiming that they grant the patriarch of Constantinople the right to receive appeals from clergy not only from churches subject to him, but also from other Patriarchal Thrones and local Autocephalous Churches which do not belong to his ecclesiastical jurisdiction. These canons of the Fourth Ecumenical Council state: "And if a clergyman have a complaint against his own or any other bishop, let it be decided by the synod of the province. And if a bishop or clergyman should have a difference with the metropolitan of the province, let him have recourse to the Exarch of the Diocese, or to the throne of the Imperial City of Constantinople, and there let it be tried."[80]

Almost all distinguished theologians and specialist canonists point out that both Canons 9 and 17 of the Fourth Ecumenical Council offer two equal options. That is to say, a member of the clergy can appeal either to the exarch of the Diocese or to the archbishop of Constantinople. The canons provide the possibility of an equally valid appeal, and therefore do not grant the archbishop of Constantinople supreme juridical responsibility or a larger degree of jurisdiction.

At this point we consider it appropriate to quote the entire extensive commentary of St Nikodimos the Hagiorite on Canon 9 of the Fourth Ecumenical Council, since we think that only this very detailed commentary is sufficient to convince even the most skeptical readers that the ecumenical patriarch does not have the canonical right to receive and adjudicate appeals from the clergy of other Orthodox Churches outside his own ecclesiastical jurisdiction.

Commenting on Canon 9 of the Fourth Ecumenical Council, St Nicodemus characteristically states that "It is clear that the Patriarch of Constantinople does not have the authority to act in the dioceses and other territories of the other Patriarchates, and this canon does not give him the right to hear appeals throughout the Church (that is, the bringing of a case from one court to another, higher court according to Book 9, Title 1 of the *Vasilika*).

i. In the fourth session of this Council of Chalcedon, Anatolios of Constantinople, who had acted outside his territory, taking Tyre from its rightful bishop Fotios and giving it to Eusebius of Beirut, deposing and excommunicating Fotios, was censured by both the civil officials and the entire Council for this. Even though he gave many excuses, everything he had done there was nevertheless declared invalid by the Council. Fotios was justified and received the bishoprics of Tyre. This is why Isaac of Ephesus told Michael, the first of the Palaiologan Emperors, that the Patriarch of Constantinople's authority does not extend to the Patriarchates of the East (according to Pachymeres, Book 6 Chapter 1).

ii. Because the civil and imperial laws do not decree that only the judgments and decisions of Constantinople are not subject to appeal, but rather the indefinite 'of each Patriarch' and plural 'of the Patriarchs'. Novel 123 of Justinian says, 'Let the Patriarch of the Diocese determine the things that accord with the ecclesiastical Canons and the laws and no party is able to object to his decision.' Leo the Wise says in Title 1 of his legal tome [the *Vasilika*], 'the Patriarch's tribunal is not subject to appeal, nor can it be retried by another, as he is the source of ecclesiastical matters, for all tribunals are from him and resolve to him.' Justinian, again, in Book 3, Chapter 2 of his ecclesiastical collection states: 'Let the competent Patriarch review the decision, without fearing an appeal'. Book 1 Title 4 of his ecclesiastical ordinance notes: 'The decisions of the Patriarchs are not appealed.' Once more, Book 1, Title 4, Chapter 29: 'It was legislated by the Emperors before us that there may not be an appeal against the decisions of the Patriarchs.' In any case, according to these Emperors, who are in agreement with the sacred canons, the decisions of all the Patriarchs are not subject to appeal and indeed they are not brought up to the tribunal of another Patriarch, so how can the Patriarch of Constantinople examine them? Whether the present canon of the Fourth Ecumenical Council, and also Canon 17 intended for the Patriarch of Constantinople to have the right to receive the appeals of the other Patriarchs, how could the Emperors have desired to establish the complete opposite at a time when they knew that civil laws not in agreement with the Canons were invalid?"[81]

Continuing his commentary on Canon 9 of the Fourth Ecumenical Council, this divinely inspired Athonite monk wrote the following:

> Therefore Zonaras too says, "The Patriarch of Constantinople by no means sits as judge of all Metropolitans, but rather of those subject to him' (interpretation of Canon 19 of the Fourth Ecumenical Council). In his interpretation of Canon 5 of Sardica, he also says, 'The Patriarch of Constantinople has the right to hear the appeals only of those subject to the Patriarch of Constantinople, just as the Pope of Rome has the right to hear the appeals only of those subject to the Pope of Rome." Now that the Synod and the Exarch of the Diocese are not active, the Patriarch of Constantinople is the first, only and last just of those Metropolitans subject to him, not of those subject to other Patriarchs.[82]

I do not think I need to further convince anyone that the ecumenical patriarch of Constantinople does not have the privilege of supreme ecclesiastical jurisdiction, and therefore does not have the right to receive and decide on appeals from bishops and clergy of Autocephalous Orthodox Churches not under his ecclesiastical jurisdiction. The distinguished canonist and Metropolitan Serafim of Pireas aptly states, "Therefore, one who has been convicted by a full Patriarchal Synod does not have the right to appeal to another Patriarchal Synod, apart from an Ecumenical Council, and it is precisely this principle that was most clearly legislated by the Holy Sixth Ecumenical Council. It was explicitly ratified in Canon 2 of the canons of the Council of Carthage which, as has been mentioned, rejected the bishop of Old Rome's claim to general jurisdiction, and consequently that of every other patriarch in the entire Church. After all, the more recent Canon 2 of the Holy Sixth Ecumenical Council definitively ratified the sacred Canons of the Council of Carthage, and, as a more recent canonical provision modifies every older one and prevails over it [the Roman legal principle *lex posterior derogat priori*], as is the case in every legal system, and as was demonstrated by the Lord's Sermon on the Mount: 'Again you have heard that it was said to those of old, "You shall not swear falsely, but shall perform your oaths to the Lord." But I say to you, do not swear' (Matthew 5:34–35)."[83]

Therefore, according to all of this, "The legal judgment expressed after the trial of a canonical case by any Holy Patriarchal Synod, which, according to our Canon Law, constitutes a complete synod, is irrevocable and can only be appealed before an ecumenical council."[84]

Based on everything we have cited so far in this chapter about the right to hear appeals, it has been clearly demonstrated that the Ecumenical Patriarchate of Constantinople has absolutely no right to receive appeals from bishops and clergy of churches not under its ecclesiastical jurisdiction. Therefore, the Holy Synod of the Ecumenical Patriarchate erroneously and anticanonically adjudicated the appeals of deposed and unordained individuals from the Ukrainian Church. It ruled on already final canonical decisions regarding former clergy of another ecclesiastical authority, and it amended and annulled decisions of the entire Patriarchal Synod of the Russian Church, which it has no authority to do.

At this point, and in view of the above, it is necessary to point out and urgently stress that the Holy Synod of the Church of Cyprus must immediately revoke Article 81 of her constitutional charter, adopted in 2010, which gives hierarchs convicted of canonical offenses the right to appeal to the Ecumenical Patriarchate, according to the provisions (it incorrectly states) of the holy canons.

This specific article reads as follows: "A hierarch who has been sentenced to defrocking, to removal from his episcopal see, or to the penalty of suspension, which may lead to expulsion, may exercise the right to appeal to the Ecumenical Patriarchate, according to the provisions of the holy canons."[85] The holy canons, however, are clear, and do not allow any misinterpretation. The Ecumenical Patriarchate of Constantinople has no right to receive appeals from outside its territory. "Only the Ecumenical Council is the final and universal judge … "[86] and therefore, the judicial decision of any autocephalous Orthodox Church can only be appealed to an ecumenical council.

The autocephalous Orthodox Church of Cyprus has the great privilege of being an Apostolic Church whose autocephaly was recognized by an ecumenical council, specifically Canon 8 of the Third Ecumenical Council of Ephesus. We deem it expedient to insert St Nikodimos's commentary of it in the *Rudder,* so that readers may more easily understand this canon. His interpretation of Canon 3 of the Third Ecumenical Council of Ephesus states the following:

> Since according to civil administration, Cyprus was subject to the Duke of Antioch, who sent a general to rule over her, the Bishop of Antioch, imitating this secular, civil model and law, wished to demonstrate that Cyprus was subject to him also, according to religious, ecclesiastical administration, and extraterritorially ordained the Bishops in Cyprus, not in keeping with the ancient custom. This is something contrary to Apostolic Canons 34 and 35. Thus, after receiving Archbishop Reginus of Constantia, which was formerly called Salamis and now Famagusta, and the bishops with him, Zeno of Cyrene and Evagrius of Soli, who reported these things in letters and verbally, the Council establishes through the present Canon that according to the Canons and according to ancient custom the Metropolitans of Cyprus should themselves consecrate the Bishops of Cyprus and remain undisturbed and unconstrained by anyone else.[87]

The expression " … according to ancient custom," which is found both in the text of Canon 8 and in its interpretation, is used by the Holy Fathers of the Third Ecumenical Council because, as stated in the Commentary by St Nicodemus the Hagiorite:

> ... previously, and from the beginning, Cyprus was established by ancient custom as autocephalous in ecclesiastical administration. This privilege was ratified for her both by the Emperor Zeno and Justinian II. In Zeno's time, the Eutychian Monophysites were prospering, and the then patriarch of Antioch, Peter Fullo was striving to subject the Cypriots, claiming that the Cypriots had received the faith from Antioch. It so happened, however, that the then bishop of Famagusta, Anthemios, received a revelation, and through it found the relics of the Holy Apostle Barnabas under the roots of a carob tree. The apostle's relics were holding the Gospel of Mark to his chest, a copy written in Greek by the hands of the apostle Barnabas himself. This happened for two reasons: first, so that the followers of Eutyches would be confounded by this divine Gospel, as it makes Christ's true humanity and two natures clear, and second, so that the tormentor of the Cypriots, Peter, would be silenced. For the holy apostle Barnabas told Anthemios, "If your enemies say that the patriarchal throne of Antioch is Apostolic, you tell them that Cyprus too is Apostolic, since she has an Apostle on her land." Taking the Gospel, Anthemios left for Constantinople and went directly to Emperor Zeno, who, upon seeing the gospel, rejoiced greatly, and, keeping it, ordered that it be read every year on Good Friday, according to the Chronicle of Joel. Not only did he appoint Akakios to review the case between the Cypriots and the Antiochians (in which Anthemios, presenting the canon of the Third Ecumenical Council and the words of the Apostle Barnabas, put the Antiochians to shame), but he also made Famagusta an archbishopric, free from the influence of Antioch, according to the monk Cyril, the reader Theodoros

Anagnostes and the Suda. According to Balsamon, Justinian II beautifully renovated Famagusta, or Salamis, and named it New Justiniana.[88]

We see, then, that the issue of administratively subordinating the Church of Cyprus to the jurisdiction of the Patriarchate of Antioch was inextricably linked to securing the canonical right to consecrate the bishops of Cyprus. In Canon 3, the Third Ecumenical Council ratified the autocephalous status of the Church of Cyprus precisely by refusing to grant Antioch the right to consecrate, and, consequently, to judge the bishops of Cyprus. It is a canonical fact that the right to consecrate bishops (*jus ordinandi*) and the right to judge bishops (*jus jurandi*) determine a Church's autocephaly or dependence on the jurisdiction of another. That is, if a Church has the right to both consecrate and judge her bishops, then she is fully autocephalous. If, however, she does not have this right, then she is not autocephalous, but rather subordinate to the ecclesiastical jurisdiction of another. Once more, if a Church does not have this twofold right, that is, to consecrate and to judge her bishops, but instead only has one of them, either the right to consecrate her bishops or the right to judge them, then her autocephaly is not full, but rather truncated, mutilated, and incomplete.

It thus becomes clear from all the documents that we have cited, that if we do not revoke Article 81 of the Charter of the Church of Cyprus, which gives Cypriot bishops the right to appeal to the Ecumenical Patriarchate, then it is as though we have accepted that the autocephaly of the Church of Barnabas is not full, but rather incomplete, since the right to judge her bishops is not held by the Holy Synod of the Church of Cyprus, but rather by the Ecumenical Patriarchate of Constantinople. In this case, it would constitute a tragic contradiction, since with the new Charter we have increased the number of hierarchical eparchies to ten and the members of the Holy Synod to seventeen in order to preserve our autocephaly intact (since Cyprus will be able to judge her bishops on her own, without having to resort to neighboring patriarchates to provide the canonically stipulated number of twelve bishops required to adjudicate a serious case involving a bishop), while at the same time ourselves mutilating and truncating this autocephaly with the adoption and acceptance of Article 81 of the Charter of our Most Holy Church, which gives our bishops the right to appeal to the Ecumenical Patriarchate, which will have the final word, since its decisions will be final, definitive, and irrevocable.

I am certain that if the present gathering of the Holy Synod of the Saint-bearing Church of the apostle Barnabas does not annul this controversial and anticanonical article, in this way healing her mutilated autocephaly, a later gathering of the Holy Synod of the Apostolic Church of Cyprus will do so.

Returning, however, to our topic, we will conclude by noting that the Holy Synod of the Ecumenical Patriarchate not only adjudicated appeals without any right to do so, but also repealed the deposal of Filaret Denisenko and his schismatic group without the necessary preconditions set by the holy canons. Canon 8 of the First Ecumenical Council and Canons 4 and 7 of the Second Ecumenical Council define the manner of admitting and integrating those coming from heresies or, as in this case, schisms, back into ecclesiastical communion. On the basis of what these canons stipulate, in order for the restoration of ecclesiastical communion with schismatics to be valid:

i) There must be an expression of repentance and sorrow on the part of the schismatics.

ii) There must be a willingness, on the part of the schismatics, to return to the Church from which they split, because the restoration of communion with the whole of Orthodoxy takes place through the restoration of communion with their local Church. In this way, the local Church is not disregarded, and the basic and fundamental principle of ecclesiological tradition, according to which a conviction for ecclesiastical offenses in a local church is valid throughout the whole of the Orthodox Church, is not violated.

iii) As former schismatics, they must be subject to the canonical bishops, "so that there will not be two bishops in the same city."[89]

In regard to those who received ordination from the self-consecrated, unordained, Makary Maletich and his group, one may reasonably wonder: How can the priesthood of self-consecrated individuals be validated? Can the Ecumenical Patriarch alone cure the absence of apostolic succession with an Act? Should not both Makary and his group have been re-ordained? After all this, "with what inner episcopal conscience can a Bishop endeavor to recognize such 'ordinations'? This is not a doubt about the moral purity of certain individuals, but rather the ontological non-existence of the very innermost core of Episcopacy. We do not have a moral, but rather an ontological 'contamination' of the Episcopal Body at a pan-Orthodox level."[90]

The Interruption
of Eucharistic Communion
between Orthodox Churches

There is another issue that we should not fail to clarify; the issue of the interruption of Eucharistic communion between two Orthodox Churches.

Some accuse the Patriarchate of Moscow of having broken Eucharistic communion with the Ecumenical Patriarchate of Constantinople and, later, with the Churches of Greece and Alexandria (or at least with those of their Bishops who received and concelebrated with clergy of the schismatic groups of the Ukrainian Church) in a hasty and theologically impermissible manner.

These recent critics of the Patriarchate of Moscow forget, or would like to forget, that the leading master of this method is Ecumenical Patriarch Bartholomew himself. We should never forget that pompous ceremony at the Phanar, televised worldwide, where the ecumenical patriarch and many metropolitans of the Ecumenical Throne imposed a penalty of *akoinonisia* (being forbidden from receiving Holy Communion) upon His Beatitude Archbishop Christodoulos of Athens and all Greece. This was all because His Beatitude dared to convene the hierarchy of the Church of Greece, which elected, without patriarchal decree, three new metropolitans to eparchies of the so-called New Lands.

[The New Lands are the new territories that were annexed to the Kingdom of Greece following the Balkan Wars,[91] on the basis of the July 28, 1913 Treaty of Bucharest. They were called "New Countries" in contrast to the "old" territories, which belonged to Greece prior to the Balkan Wars. These new territories are Macedonia, part of Epirus, the islands of the northern and eastern Aegean (Thasos, Samothrace, Lemnos, Lesbos, Chios, Samos, Ikaria), and Crete. After the Asia Minor catastrophe and the new tragic situation created and finalized by the 1923 Treaty of Lausanne,[92] the Turks decided to issue the notorious December 6, 1923 *Tezkire* of the Municipality of Istanbul, which stipulated that from then on, both the patriarch and the members of the Patriarchal Synod must be Turkish nationals[93] and serve on Turkish territory. Moreover, according to the *Tezkire*, the metropolitans of the New Lands could no longer participate in the Synod or on Synodal councils of the Ecumenical Patriarchate. In order to avoid undesirable developments (such as potential schismatic activity by the metropolitans of the New Lands) the Ecumenical Patriarchate was forced to resolve the issue with the Patriarchal and Synodical Act of 1928. The Act conditionally and *epitropikos* [in trust] transferred the administration of the twenty-six metropoles of the New Lands and the election of their metropolitans to the Church of Greece, thus ensuring their participation in the Synod of the Church of Greece.[94]]

Indeed, at the time, did any of the primates or other hierarchs condemn this action against His Beatitude Archbishop

Christodoulos? Was that not a case of suspending Eucharistic communion, not for reasons of faith or dogma, but for reasons of authority and jurisdiction? Why was there such indifference then? Why is there such sensitivity now? Let us also not forget the Ecumenical Patriarchate's temporary suspension of Eucharistic communion with the Patriarchate of Jerusalem, or overlook the unfortunate, ongoing Eucharistic suspension between the Patriarchates of Antioch and Jerusalem.

We all agree that the nature and essence of the Orthodox Church in its fullness is participation in Eucharistic communion. We can also agree that the sacrament of the Divine Eucharist, and shared participation in it, expresses the visible unity of the Body of the Church, and constitutes the culmination of communion of brother with brother. The Divine Eucharist, this greatest Mystery of Mysteries, must therefore remain, as much as possible, removed from any ecclesiastical dispute which is not primarily regarding dogmatic issues or issues of faith in general. However, when the holy canons are violated, and a deviation from timeless ecclesiastical canonical practice and tradition is observed, a suspension of Eucharistic communion must be imposed until the reasons that necessitated it are removed.

The Orthodox Patriarchate of Moscow suspended Eucharistic communion with the Ecumenical Patriarchate of Constantinople on account of the latter's violation of the holy canons. As we have demonstrated above, the ecumenical patriarch's unilateral intervention in the Church of Ukraine, which is not his canonical territory, culminated in the anticanonical grant of a Tome of Autocephaly to schismatic groups in that country. The Patriarchate of Moscow also suspended communion with the Orthodox Churches of Greece and Alexandria, because they officially recognized the anticanonical actions of the Ecumenical Patriarchate in accepting the unrepentant Ukrainian schismatics into communion. So, the unity of the primates was not divided for petty and ethnophyletic reasons, nor was the commemoration of the ecumenical patriarch suspended due to secondary trivialities, as some suggest. Both were done for reasons of legal and canonical ethics of conduct.

One of the basic principles of the Canon Law of the Orthodox Church is that if someone receives an excommunicated individual into Eucharistic communion, then he himself is excommunicated. The sacred canons condemn those who receive deposed or excommunicated individuals into prayerful communion, or concelebrate with them. Apostolic Canon 10 stipulates: "If someone prays together with an excommunicated person, even at home, let him be cast out."[95]

Likewise, Apostolic Canon 11 stipulates: "If someone prays with a deposed member of the clergy as though he is a member of the clergy, let him too be deposed."[96]

Additionally, Canon 5 of the First Ecumenical Council notes that " … those who have been cast out by some may not be readmitted by others."[97]

Lastly, Canon 2 of the Council of Antioch stresses that "If a bishop, presbyter, deacon or anyone of the Canon is found to commune with excommunicated persons, he too is excommunicated, as having confounded the canon of the

Church."[98] Therefore, "any Bishop, Presbyter, or Deacon who willingly communed with such excommunicated persons, whether at home or at Church, himself becomes excommunicated by the others, for what he does violates and confounds the canons of the Church appointed in this regard, namely, Apostolic Canons 10 and 11."[99]

These are the holy canons which required the Orthodox Patriarchate of Moscow to suspend Eucharistic communion with the Ecumenical Patriarchate of Constantinople, the primates of the Orthodox Churches of Greece and Alexandria, and all those hierarchs who received representatives of the Ukrainian schismatics into communion.

Therefore, the Orthodox Patriarchate of Moscow's decision to suspend Eucharistic communion with the three aforementioned Churches is correct and justified, because it is grounded in the holy canons, and in accordance with ecclesiastical practice through the ages.

Who Is the Head of the One, Holy, Catholic, and Apostolic Church?

The most concerning thing currently happening in regard to the Ukrainian ecclesiastical issue is the fact that it is evolving into a major ecclesiological problem, since the ambitions of the Ecumenical Patriarchate are now extended to the entire Church, as it claims the right to intervene in the internal affairs of all the local Orthodox Patriarchates and Autocephalous Churches. As he notes in his letter to Archbishop Anastasios of Albania, he [the ecumenical patriarch] demands to intervene across jurisdictional boundaries throughout the Orthodox church, "*ex officio* and out of obligation": " ... not only in cases of Doctrine, holy Tradition, and Canonical Church Regulations, or even of general matters concerning the entire body of the Church, but also in all matters pertaining to important issues of specific interest to one or another Local Church."[100]

These attempts by the Patriarchate of Constantinople to arrogate rights which belong exclusively to the whole Church are explicitly expressed in the so-called Tome which the Ecumenical Patriarchate issued and handed over to Epiphany on January 6, 2019, during the Divine Liturgy for the feast of the Theophany at the Phanar. Commenting on this Tome in his study on the issue, emeritus professor of Canon Law at the University of Athens, Panagiotis Boumis wrote the following:

> Further in the fourth paragraph it is written: "In addition to the above, we declare that the Autocephalous Church in Ukraine knows as its head the most holy Apostolic and Patriarchal Ecumenical Throne, just as the rest of the patriarchs and primates also do." And one wonders: how is it declared without a doubt that an Autocephalous Church recognizes "the Ecumenical Throne as its head" and how can it be said that the other patriarchs do so? Especially when among "the other patriarchs", are the primates of the ancient Patriarchates?[101]

Church historians and scholars have noted that none of the Tomes of Autocephaly issued by the Ecumenical Patriarchate to churches within its in its ecclesiastical jurisdiction in the last 170 years (Greece, 1850; Serbia, 1879; Romania, 1885; Poland, 1924; Albania, 1937; Bulgaria, 1945; Czech Lands and Slovakia, 1998) claim that the Ecumenical Patriarchate of Constantinople is their head.

Unfortunately, this novel theory that the Church of Constantinople is the Head of all the Churches receives the support and cooperation of certain members of the Ecumenical See, who, misinterpreting Apostolic Canon 34, stress that according to this canon, someone among the primates should be considered "First" and "Head" of the rest. Among the supporters of this novel and insipid theory is the very dear, respected, and distinguished canonist, Theodore Giagkos, dean of the Theological School of the Aristotle University of Thessaloniki, and a member, under my presidency, of the

Synodal Committee on Canonical Issues of the Church of Cyprus. In his recent study on the Autocephaly of the Church in Ukraine, Giagkos notes the following: "While at the level of local Churches the institution of conciliarity is defined by the constitutional Charters, in Pan-Orthodox conciliar institutions, where the responsibilities of the *Protos* [first] are sufficiently defined, the Protos, as well as his responsibilities, are treated with skepticism."[102] He continues:

> The institution of synods, according to the canons, principally functions harmoniously when the position of the Protos is accepted by the members of the synod. "[They] account him as their head, and do nothing of consequence without his consent." Of course, in the East we do not have a Pope, **but we do have a Protos who has the responsibilities of the Head** [emphasis my own]. This means that above all, he possesses precedence when solving the problems that concern the Churches acting and deciding together with the members of the synod. "But neither let him do anything without the consent of all." The praise of the Triune God comes forth from the harmony (unanimity) of conciliarity. "For so there will be unity, and God will be glorified through the Lord in the Holy Spirit" (Apostolic Canon 34). At the level of the local Churches the above fundamental conciliar principles are applied without much doubt. In contrast, at the pan-Orthodox level, there is often reluctance to respect the institution of the Protos.[103]

The issue, then, of the Ecumenical Patriarchate's leadership, as expressed in the so-called Ukrainian Tome of Autocephaly, as well as in the arguments of certain members of the

Ecumenical See, raises the question of who is the Head of the One, Holy, Catholic, and Apostolic Church.

Historically and canonically, the answer regarding the leadership of the Church is one and indisputable. Over the course of her 2000-year history, the Orthodox Church did not entrust any of her bishops with the title and responsibilities of head of the Church. Apostolic Canon 34's concept of a "Head," which is applied to the "First" of the eparchial synod, is mistakenly transmuted to a universal headship, in order to justify a universal protos as "Head" of the "Firsts" of the universal Church, something that cannot be accepted. St Nikodimos the Hagiorite clearly explains that "primacy at the universal level does not exist in the Church. There is only the primacy of first chair (in order of seniority or honor) among the equal primates. The primates of the local Orthodox Churches are equal in honor according to the 'privileges of honor' and differ only according to the order of honor."[104]

Concerning the same subject, Dositheos of Jerusalem writes: "There are many major parishes, there are many [Orthodox] Churches, there are many Leaders, church Presidents, and Archons, but none among them is the Leader of Leaders, the President of Presidents, the Archon of Archons. Among those Archons, Leaders, and Presidents, the bishop of Rome is equal in honor, equal in authority, and nothing more."[105]

The Orthodox bishop of the Eparchy of Zara in Dalmatia, His Eminence, Doctor of Canon Law Nikodim Milaš, whose knowledge and prestige is universally recognized in the Orthodox world, dealt with the issue seriously. Living around the end of the nineteenth century, he composed his famous and weighty volume, *The Ecclesiastical Law of the Eastern Orthodox Church*. In this work, he makes the following very interesting comments:

> When Christ founded the Church on earth, he gave all His Apostles equal authority in her (Matthew 18:17–20, 28:19–20; John 20:21–22). However, he retained the ultimate governance of the Church for Himself, calling Himself the head of the shepherds and the only True Shepherd (John 10:14–16). When the issue was stirred up among the Apostles as to who among them has privileges of honor, Christ condemned the very notion of this (Matthew 20:22–27, 23:8–12; Mark 9:34–35, 10:42–45; I Peter 5:2–4), saying that He is the only Head of His salvific Kingdom, His Church (John 18:36; I Peter 5:4; Hebrews 13:20).

He then highlights the following, written by the Apostle Paul: "The husband is head of the wife, as also Christ is head of the church; and He is the Savior of the body" (Ephesians 5:23). And again: "He put all things under His feet, and gave Him to be head over all things to the church, which is His body, the fullness of Him who fills all in all" (Ephesians 1:22–23). In his Epistle to the Colossians, he also states: "And He is the head of the body, the church, who is the beginning, the firstborn from the dead, that in all things He may have the preeminence" (Colossians 1:18).

This most wise hierarch, Nikodim Milaš, again points out:

> The acts of the Apostles most certainly confirm this (Acts 1:21–26, 6:2–6, 15:1–29) and the Apostle Paul, seeing some who were attempting to establish privileges of honor in the Church,

criticizes this tendency in scathing terms (Galatians 2:6–14). In later centuries, the Fathers of the Church confirm this: Basil the Great (Preface on the Judgment of God, number 3): "The one and only true head, that is, Christ ... prevailing"; Gregory the Theologian (Logos 31): "The One Christ is the one Head of the Church", Gregory of Nyssa (Logos 12, Against Eunomios), Theodoret of Cyrus (Commentary on the Epistle to the Ephesians 1:23), Theophylact (Commentary on I Corinthians 11:3). Today, the Eastern Orthodox Church confesses this teaching with the following statement: "Only Christ is the head of the Church (Ephesians 5:23, Colossians 1:18)." Therefore, if in the Churches their leading hierarchs are called their heads, this should be understood as meaning that they are individually Christ's stewards within His own eparchy, and partial heads (Acts 20:28). The head of the shepherds is, according to the Apostle Peter (I Peter 5:4), Jesus Christ alone (Orthodox Confession, Part I, Question 85). "For no mortal man can be the universal and eternal head of any universal Church. Our Lord Jesus Christ Himself is the head and He, at the helm of governance in the Church, steers her, through the Holy Fathers ... "[106]

In the same paragraph about the Church's unity, the eminent bishop of Zara points out:

If the Church, as is true, is a spiritual kingdom, her unity and oneness, is and should be, spiritual ... As a spiritual kingdom, the Church cannot have an earthly, visible head in whom the Church's whole authority coalesces, because the Church's divine founder enveloped all His Apostles in the right and discipline of authority. All of the bishops necessarily share the same authority, inasmuch as they are successors of the Apostles and leaders of different local Churches.[107]

We must stress, however, that the dogmatically clearest answer was given by the Apostle Paul, and it is the one that Milaš emphasizes: " … And He put all things under His feet, and gave Him to be head over all things to the church, which is His body, the fullness of Him who fills all in all" (Ephesians 1:22–23).

It is therefore clearly evident, documented historically, canonically, dogmatically, scripturally, and patristically, that none of the primates, patriarchs, or presidents of Autocephalous Churches can replace the only timeless Head of the Church, Our Lord Jesus Christ.

The Church, in her conciliarity and catholicity, has no head other than our Lord Jesus Christ. It is the Ecumenical Councils which exercise supreme canonical authority in the Church, not any primate.

The Church has always believed that an ecumenical council is the only infallible and supreme institution, and has ecclesiologically interpreted it as such. St Nikodimos the Hagiorite stresses this: "As we have said, only the Ecumenical Council is the final and universal Judge of all the Patriarchs, and none other."[108]

Therefore, any ambitious primate of an Orthodox Church owes it to himself to always remember the answer that Christ gave to James and John, sons of Zebedee, when they asked for primacy, provoking the other disciples to resent them: "But Jesus called them to Himself and said to them, 'You know that those who are considered rulers over the Gentiles lord it over them, and their great ones exercise authority over them. Yet it shall not be so among you; but whoever desires to become great among you shall be your servant. And whoever of you desires to be first shall be slave of all'" (Mark 10:42–44).

The author of the Patriarchal Encyclical of 1895 certainly kept all the above in mind when, responding to an invitation to union from the pope of Rome, succinctly confuted all the false papal teachings by writing the following about the "primacy" of the pope:

> But having recourse to the Fathers and the Ecumenical Councils of the Church of the first nine centuries, we are certain that the bishop of Rome was never considered the highest principal and infallible head of the Church, and that each bishop is head and president of his own individual Church, subject only to the synodal decrees and decisions of the universal Church. The councils do not exempt the bishop of Rome from this rule, and do not say that only his commands and decisions are infallible. As ecclesiastical history shows, the only eternal leader and immortal head of the Church is our Lord Jesus Christ ... [109]

We should mention that this Encyclical is signed by then Ecumenical Patriarch Anthimos, as well as twelve other metropolitans of the Ecumenical See.

I believe that with all these substantive arguments mentioned above, the novel theory that the ecumenical patriarch is the head of the universal Orthodox Church is, both canonically and dogmatically, rebutted.

The Tradition of the Great Endemic Synod of Constantinople

I honestly wonder whether this claim of monarchical rights over the entire Church is the reason Ecumenical Patriarch Bartholomew avoided convening a synod of the primates of all the Orthodox Churches (in order to obtain their opinion and consent) before issuing the Ukrainian Tome of Autocephaly. Having avoided the synod, however, why did he not at least follow the established canonical tradition which has been used by his predecessors since the Great Schism of 1054, and, more generally, during the difficult post-Byzantine times, the Great Endemic Synod in Constantinople?

It is well known that "after the Great Schism (1054) and the installation of Latin Crusader hierarchs in the Patriarchates of Antioch and Jerusalem and the Church of Cyprus, when dealing with serious matters of faith or canonical order, patriarchs and hierarchs living in Constantinople were invited to and participated in the Patriarchal Synod."[110] According to Professor Vlasios Fidas, this synod was called an Endemic Synod, and was considered to be in accordance with the exceptional privileges of the See of Constantinople as the "first see in the East."[111]

Indeed, according to Fidas, the Great Endemic Synod was an enlarged version of the Synod of the Ecumenical Patriarchate.

Patriarchs of the East, or their representatives, who lived in Constantinople were invited and participated, always under the presidency of the ecumenical patriarch, in order to deal with serious issues of faith or canonical order which threatened the unity of the Church. The validity of the decisions of these Great Endemic Constantinopolitan Synods was important and indisputable, as they had the consent of the other ancient Patriarchates of the East. Great Endemic Synods were convened for, inter alia:

i. Renouncing the Council of Florence (1484),

ii. Condemning the Calvinist Confession of Faith attributed to Ecumenical Patriarch Cyril Loukaris (1638, 1642, 1672, 1691),

iii. Addressing the complicated Sinai Issue (1575, 1615, 1645, 1648, 1670),

iv. Evaluating the Anglican non-Jurors (1718, 1723, 1727),

v. Condemning ethnophyletic agitations in the Bulgarian Exarchate (1872),[112] etc.

We should particularly remember that a Great Endemic Synod was convened in Constantinople in 1590 to ratify Ecumenical Patriarch Jeremias II's 1589 decision to elevate the Metropolis of Moscow to a Patriarchate by a patriarchal chrysobull. Indeed, four years later, in 1594, another Great Endemic Synod was convened to express its consent to the election of the new patriarch of Alexandria, Meletios Pigas.

I am certain that if His All-Holiness Ecumenical Patriarch Bartholomew had done this in the case of Ukraine, he would have avoided many mistakes, and his position on the issue of Ukrainian autocephaly would doubtless be stronger.

The Conciliar and Hierarchical System of Governance of the Universal Orthodox Church

Since we have repeatedly referred to the Orthodox Church's conciliar, collective, and democratic system of governance, in contrast to the Roman Catholic Church's monarchical and absolutely centralized papal administrative system, we would be remiss if we did not treat, if briefly, the Orthodox conciliar system of governance.

The ancient and undivided Church had a profound consciousness of being the mystical body of Christ. She recognized that she is one and indivisible, a divine and human, visible and invisible organism, whose one sole Head, her divine Founder, our Lord Jesus Christ, based her entire organization on this basic principle. Thus, the early Church found the form for her system of governance not in a monarchical, authoritarian system, but in the conciliar collective which is the Ecumenical Council. This form of governance, fully corresponding to the essence and mission of the Church as the spiritual and supernatural organism par excellence, harmonized the Church's human factor with her divine magnitude, placing the human in a position of submission to the divine, and revealing the divine as the Church's supreme principal.[113]

Therefore, the one, undivided Church before the Great Schism had as her supreme collective body the Ecumenical Council. This conciliar system of administration was received and continued by the later Church. The Ecumenical Council was and is the supreme legislative, administrative, and judicial body, both of the early, pre-schism, undivided Church, and of its successor, the universal Orthodox Church. The Ecumenical Councils both defined the dogmas of the Church and regulated the fundamental principles of ecclesiastical organization.

It must also be stressed and clarified:

While in the eyes of the law the Ecumenical Council constitutes the highest collective body of Church governance, its decisions are nevertheless subject to the control of the "Ecclesiastical Conscience", the unanimous, common, opinion of the clergy and laity, which, even if it cannot be defined in an organic expression, is the highest power over the Ecumenical Councils, whose final characterization as Ecumenical does not depend so much on their being convened, as on their being recognized as Ecumenical by the Church's conscience. This high significance and importance that the "Ecclesiastical Conscience" possesses in the formation of the Ecclesiastical System of Governance is, so to speak, the culmination of basic democratic principles which regulated the system of governance of the early and undivided Church. That is to say, it is not the will of one person ... that constitutes the source of ecclesiastical authority, in terms of law, but rather the will of the body of the Hierarchy, which gradually, through the Bishops and district heads, and following Patriarchal and indeed, Ecumenical Councils, is referred to the Church's divine Head, so that Christ may "be all and in all" (cf. Colossians 3:11). In this way, the Church's primary spiritual and otherworldly character is exalted, and the living conviction of the believers is that in reality, the single, true

Governor of the Church is the Lord himself, and the hierarchy is merely the instrument through which the Church's governance is authentically achieved and upheld.[114]

This conciliar system, which constitutes the system of governance of the universal Orthodox Church, and which culminates in the institution of the Ecumenical Council, is only convened when there is a need for all the Churches to jointly decide on an issue. This does not happen for the local affairs of a particular Church, but for important and serious issues which concern Orthodoxy as a whole, i.e., matters of faith (dogmas, heresies), ecclesiastical organization (canons), and other things.

The foundations upon which this Conciliar system is based were laid by the Apostles themselves. Panagiotis Boumis, Emeritus Professor of the University of Athens, notes that "conciliarity appears in, and is prescribed by, the Acts of the Apostles." In Chapter 15 we see the following expressions of it:

i) "It pleased the apostles and elders, with the whole church … " (Verse 22)

ii) "It seemed good to us, being assembled with one accord … " (Verse 25)

iii) "It seemed good to the Holy Spirit, and to us … " (Verse 28)[115]

Certain expressions found in passages in the book of Acts not only ensure the documentation of a conciliar system of governance, but also show a hierarchical system of governance, since the Orthodox Church's system of governance is not only conciliar, but also hierarchical. Thus, in Chapter 15 of the Acts of the Apostles, we see the following expressions, which indicate the hierarchical nature of the Orthodox Church's conciliar system of governance:

i) "Now the apostles and elders came together to consider this matter" (Verse 6).

ii) "And when there had been much dispute, Peter rose up and said to them … " (Verse 7)

iii) "Then all the multitude kept silent and listened to Barnabas and Paul declaring how many miracles and wonders God had worked through them among the Gentiles" (Verse 12).

iv) "And after they had become silent, James answered, saying … " (Verse 13)[116]

From these passages from the Acts of the Apostles, we can discern the authority and responsibility of the Apostles-Hierarchs for making conciliar decisions. At this Apostolic Council, four Apostles who were highly regarded in the conciliar assembly took the floor as hierarchs and pastors: Peter, Paul, Barnabas, and James.

The fact, however, that the Orthodox Church's system of administration is Conciliar-Hierarchal, is also evident from certain passages from the Holy Fathers. We will mention St John Chrysostom, who, interpreting Psalm 149:1 "His praise in the church of the saints," wrote "It shows that worship should be offered up together and with all concord, for 'Church' is a name for system and council."[117]

Nikodim Milaš adds, "However, while the organ of the highest ecclesiastical authority over the entire Church is the Ecumenical Council, in specific Churches, this organ is the local synod."[118]

The institution of the local synod was instituted and legislated by the divine and holy canons. Apostolic Canon 37 stipulates, "Let there be a synod of bishops twice a year, once in the fourth week of Pentecost and once in the month of October, and together let them closely examine the teachings of the faith, and let them resolve the ecclesiastical disputes that have arisen."[119] In his commentary on this canon, Nicodemus the Hagiorite informs us that "the timing of one of these two synods was changed by Canon 5 of the First Ecumenical Council, so that it convenes before Holy Lent, so that by means of the Synod's judgment, every difference and partiality that the clergy and laity might have towards each other and toward their Bishop may be dispelled from their midst, and thus they may purely and passionlessly offer God the gift of the fast."[120]

Indeed, Canon 5 of the First Ecumenical Council states, "Let the synods take place as so: one before Lent, so that all meanness of spirit having been put away, the pure gift may be offered to God; the second, around the time of autumn."[121]

On the same topic, Canon 19 of the Fourth Ecumenical Council, Canon 8 of the Sixth Ecumenical Council, and Canon 6 of the Seventh Ecumenical Council all refer to the convening of local synods. Canon 19 of the Fourth Ecumenical Council states: "The holy Council has therefore stipulated, in accordance with the canons of the Holy Fathers, that the Bishops meet twice a year somewhere in each province, wherever the Bishop of the Metropolis deems appropriate, and set aright all matters that arise. Those bishops who do not take part and remain in their own cities, if they are in good health and free of any indispensable and necessary occupation, are to be fraternally rebuked."[122]

That is to say, this canon makes the bishops' attendance at two annual synods mandatory, and stipulates that bishops who are unjustifiably absent should be reprimanded. After adopting the decisions relating to local synods established by the Holy Fathers of the previous councils, Canon 8 of the Sixth Ecumenical Council differs with regard to the number of times they are to be convened annually, stating the following: "Since, on account of barbarian raids and other causes that arise, the Presidents of the Churches are unable to hold Synods twice a year, it has seemed best for the aforementioned Bishops to convene a synod once a year, as is reasonable, for those ecclesiastical matters that arise in every province, from the holy feast of Pascha to the end of the month of October of each year, in the place which the Bishop of the Metropolis, as has been said, deems appropriate."[123]

Finally, Canon 6 of the Seventh Ecumenical Council renews the decision of Canon 8 of the Sixth Ecumenical Council, which stipulates that one synod take place a year on account of insurmountable difficulties due to barbarian raids. This canon, however, adds that any ruler who prevents the synod from being convened should be excommunicated, and that any metropolitan who neglects to do this—that is, to convene the synod once a year—should be punished with penalties. It specifically mentions that "… the Holy Fathers of the Sixth Council stipulated that it should convene once a year, by any means and through any pretext, and set aright those things that have gone wrong. Therefore, we renew this canon, and if a ruler is found to be hindering this, let him be excommunicated. If any Metropolitan does not attend, apart from cases of necessity, violence, or some reasonable excuse, let him be subject to penalties."[124]

Canon 20 of the Council of Antioch also deals with this same issue, as does Canon 40 of the Council of Laodicea.

The basis, however, for the functions of the conciliar and hierarchical system of governance in local Churches is Apostolic Canon 34, which states that the metropolitan of each province is bound to honor the authority of his bishops. They should not do anything that goes beyond the boundaries of their bishoprics without his consent, while he himself should not do anything without the consent of all the bishops. In this manner, the conciliar and hierarchical system of governance of each local Church is made evident. Apostolic Canon 34 decrees as follows: "The bishops of each nation must acknowledge the first among them and hold him as the head, and do nothing extraordinary without his consent. Each must only do those things which concern his own parish and the rural areas dependent on it. But neither may he do anything without the consent of all, for in this way there will be unanimity and God will be glorified, through the Lord and in the Holy Spirit: the Father, the Son and the Holy Spirit."[125]

In order for everyone to understand the content of this canon, we think it is appropriate to quote its interpretation as it is found in the *Rudder*, which reads as follows:

> All the Bishops of each province should recognize the one who is first among them, that is the Metropolitan, and they should consider him as their head. Without his consent, they should not

do anything extra-jurisdictional: that is, anything that does not pertain to the parishes within their Bishoprics, but rather going beyond them, regards an issue common to the entire province, for example, issues regarding questions of dogmas, applications of economy, corrections of collective faults, the situations and consecrations of Bishops, and other similar things. Rather, they should convene with their Metropolitan and consult with him about these matters, and whatever solution seems best to them should be decided in common. On his own, without consulting his Metropolitan, each bishop should only do those things which pertain to the parishes of his bishopric and to the rural areas subject to his Bishopric. Likewise, the Bishops should not do anything collectively without the consent of the Metropolitan, and the Metropolitan should not do something on his own without the consent of all the Bishops. For through this practice, there will be unanimity and love between the Bishops, the Metropolitan, the Clergy, and the Laity. For this unanimity and love intends for God the Father to be glorified through His Son, our Lord Jesus Christ, who revealed to humans the name of the Father, and legislated love, saying, "By this all will know that you are My disciples, if you have love for one another" (John 13:35). It also intends for Him to be glorified in the Holy Spirit, who by His grace united us in one spiritual union. That is to say, according to the words of the Gospel, "Let your light so shine before men, that they may see your good works and glorify your Father in heaven" (Matthew 5:16).[126]

This apostolic canon shows a wonderful balance, through which unity may prevail in the Church, both in specific local Churches and in the entire Ecumenical Church. We should make it clear that according to this canon the bishops of each province should recognize the metropolitan (primate) as first among them, consider him to be their head, and not do anything extra-jurisdictional—i.e., anything that transcends the boundaries of their dioceses and concerns the entire regional Church—without his consent. This does not, however, give the protos the right to abuse this honor, and intervene, without the consent and permission of his bishops, in the internal affairs of their bishoprics. According to Anastasios Vavouskos, "Within their geographical area, the shepherding Bishop is the all-powerful and indisputable leader while he is alive and able to perform his pastoral duties (see Canon 16 of the Protodeutera Council of Constantinople in 861), conduct the administration of his diocese, and handle its affairs."[127] In his commentary on Apostolic Canon 34, St Nicodemus the Hagiorite specifically emphasizes the following: "This is why John of Kitros says that if the Metropolitan celebrates the liturgy in the Bishopric of a Bishop, he should do so with the consent and permission of that Bishop. In the diptychs, however, he should commemorate the name of the Patriarch, and not that of his Bishop, since it is strange for the greater to refer to the name of the lesser, according to Harmenopoulos' compendium of the canons."[128]

Having said this, we cannot fail to point out the fault in the new Charter of the Church of Cyprus concerning the rights of her primates. In Article 12, Paragraph 9, the archbishop is given the right to "officiate in all of Cyprus, **by simply announcing his intent to do so to the local Hierarch**" (emphasis is my own)[129] The novel phrase, "by simply announcing his intent to do so to the local Hierarch," is contrary to the sacred canons and the tradition of the Orthodox Church, and, furthermore, is completely unnecessary. Therefore, it would be good for it to be removed.

Concluding this section, we stress the following: during the undivided church's foundational period, the idea and institution of a "papacy," a supreme ecclesiastic principal and source of all authority, did not exist. Before the Great Schism, the Ecumenical Council was the church's highest collective body. This conciliar system of administration was both received and continued by the Orthodox Church worldwide, so today's church governance, both ecumenically and locally, is conciliar and hierarchical. This characterization of the Orthodox Church's system of governance is confirmed by Holy Scripture, and instituted and legislated by both the holy canons and Church practice through the ages. This is why any attempt to overturn this conciliar and hierarchical system handed down by the Apostles must be avoided. The organization of the Orthodox Church is based on conciliarity, not on an absolute, monarchical, and centralizing protos. The Orthodox Catholic Church's conciliar and hierarchical system of administration must be zealously guarded if we want unity and peace in the Church.

Conclusions

Summarizing the ecclesiastical, theological, canonical, and historical facts we have so far discussed in regard to the Ukrainian question, we submit the following conclusions:

i. The Ecumenical Patriarchate of Constantinople's annulment of the 1686 Patriarchal Letter and arrogation of jurisdiction over the ecclesiastical territory of Ukraine is a unilateral, one-sided, and anticanonical act, and is therefore invalid. The ecclesiastical consciousnesses of the Ecumenical Patriarchate, the Church of Russia, and all the autocephalous churches worldwide, unhesitatingly and definitively accepted the fact that for the past 332 years (1686–2018) the Orthodox Church of Ukraine was under the ecclesiastical jurisdiction of the Patriarchate of Moscow, and constituted part of Russia's canonical territory. This pan-Orthodox ecclesiastical consensus was constantly manifested at pan-Orthodox concelebrations, conferences, irenic visits, international gatherings, and many other occasions, always without any objection or reservation.

ii. Granting of pseudo-autocephaly to schismatic groups in Ukraine without the prior knowledge and consent of the other Autocephalous Orthodox Churches, or even the Mother Church, which, in this case, is the Church of Russia, is in complete opposition to long-standing canonical tradition and timeless ecclesiastical practice, and cannot be canonically justified.

iii. One cannot repeal the ecclesiastical condemnation of deposed and anathematized individuals, unless the claimants first show a sincere and profound repentance. Reestablishment into communion cannot be achieved through an anticanonical assertion that the ecumenical patriarch of Constantinople has always had the privilege of receiving and adjudicating the appeals of clergymen from all Autocephalous Orthodox Churches worldwide. This extra-territorial claim is completely contrary to the sacred canons, which it blatantly violates. For this reason, granting autocephaly to Ukraine cannot be canonically binding, nor should it be accepted by any of the other autocephalous Churches.

iv. Anticanonically granting pseudo-autocephaly to schismatic groups in Ukraine does not restore the Ukrainian people to the canonical fold, as the ecumenical patriarch claims, since the vast majority of the Orthodox people in Ukraine remain faithful to the canonical Church under Metropolitan Onufry of Kiev and All Ukraine. Quite to the contrary, Ecumenical Patriarch Bartholomew's actions resulted in the damaging and catastrophic disintegration of the Ukrainian Church, and the painful division of her Christian body. It has caused a disastrous schism which now threatens worldwide Orthodoxy.

v. In addition to creating a major ecclesiastical problem and threatening pan-Orthodox unity with schism, the ecumenical patriarch's unilateral, one-sided, and anticanonical decision to grant autocephaly to schismatic Ukrainian ecclesiastical elements has irreparably damaged the pan-Orthodox prestige of the Ecumenical Patriarchate as coordinating center of the Orthodox Patriarchates and Autocephalous Churches.

vi. When based on dogmatic infractions or violations of the divine and holy canons, suspending Eucharistic communion between two Churches is not only permissible, but also required, both by these same holy canons and by timeless ecclesiastical practice. Therefore, the Orthodox Patriarchate of Moscow, following the holy Canons (Apostolic Canons 10 and 11, Canon 5 of the First Ecumenical Council, as well as Canon 2 of the Council of Antioch), correctly proceeded to suspend Eucharistic communion with the Ecumenical Patriarchate of Constantinople. This was done in the hope that the reasons which imposed this break in communion will be removed, and relations between the two Churches will be restored "in faith and love," with the natural result being a restoration of Eucharistic communion between them.

vii. As the Ukrainian issue progressed and developed, a new anticanonical claim came to light, namely, that in the Orthodox church, the archbishop of Constantinople and ecumenical patriarch is not "first among equals," but "first without equals." This replaces his "primacy of service" with a "primacy of authority," resulting in a violation of the principle of conciliarity which has always been practiced in the Orthodox Church.

viii. During the dangerous and unjustified ecclesiastical crisis created in the heart of Orthodoxy by the Ukrainian issue, a new doctrine appeared, claiming that the ecumenical patriarch of Constantinople is the head of the entire Orthodox Church. Misinterpreting Apostolic Canon 34, close associates of the Ecumenical Throne argue that the ecumenical patriarch should be considered the *protos* and head of all the other primates. In other words, that all patriarchs, primates, and bishops should recognize the ecumenical patriarch as the head of the universal Orthodox Church. This novel theory has no historical, canonical, dogmatic, or ecclesiological justification, because the Orthodox Church has no head other than our Lord Jesus Christ. The only eternal Leader and immortal Head of the Church is her Creator, Saviour, and Redeemer, Christ.

ix. In the case of Ukraine, the principle of conciliarity, which constitutes a fundamental element of the Orthodox Church's administration, was ignored, in favor of the principle of the unilateral and authoritarian power of the one, of Ecumenical Patriarch Bartholomew. No one can object to this fact. This is ironic, in light of historical events, as His All-Holiness presided over and coordinated the activities of the Great and Holy Council of Crete, four years ago, which proclaimed that "The Orthodox Church expresses her unity and catholicity 'in Council'. Conciliarity pervades the way she is organized, the way she makes decisions, and the path which she follows."[130]

x. Finally, we would also like to point out that "the Greek-speaking Churches, on the basis of historical truth and canonical tradition, must, in order to avoid schism, support the historical and canonical rights of the Church of Russia, and must not support, either openly or through their silence, Constantinople's anticanonical intervention in another jurisdiction. If they support the Greek patriarch out of patriotism, nationalism, or tribalism, they fall into the heresy of ethnophyletism, which was synodically condemned by Constantinople herself in 1872."[131]

Suggestions

During a conference in honor of the great theologian, Archpriest Georges Florovsky of blessed memory, His All-Holiness Patriarch Bartholomew made the following very interesting comment: "The solution to Orthodoxy's current problems can only be achieved with absolute fidelity to the tradition of the Church, and the application of theological, canonical, and ecclesiological criteria."[132] I believe that in order to solve the problematic Ukrainian ecclesiastical issue which is currently afflicting the Orthodox Church, the criteria should be precisely those stated by His All-Holiness: Orthodox Theology, Orthodox Ecclesiology, and Canonical Order. The only canonical way to restore the internal unity of the currently divided ecclesiastical body of the long-suffering Orthodox Church of Ukraine is to respect the principle of conciliarity, and to urgently convene a pan-Orthodox Council. The worldwide Orthodox Church should address, at a pan-Orthodox Council, the canonically and ecclesiologically complex Ukrainian issue. We believe a pan-Orthodox Synod is the only recourse we have in solving this difficult and thorny problem (in which geopolitical and geostrategic interests are unfortunately involved), overcoming the current crisis, and consolidating the unity of the Orthodox Catholic Church.

We are aware of all the difficulties associated with convening a pan-Orthodox Council, particularly the problem of patriarchs refusing to convene or attend, so, as a second option, we suggest a council of the primates of the Orthodox Churches. The primates of all the Autocephalous Orthodox Churches should, by applying intense pressure, convince the ecumenical patriarch to invite everyone to a gathering, a council. At this council, they should demonstrate their hierarchal wisdom, overcome their egotism, arrogance, and lust for glory, and, in a sacrificial, kenotic spirit, without disputes and conflicts, without being influenced by external political forces, or geostrategic and geopolitical interests, work to find a solution to the Ukrainian ecclesiastical issue which accords with the sacred Canons and timeless ecclesiastical practice.

If the effort to convince the "first in honor," the ecumenical patriarch, to convene a council of primates fails, then, as a third solution, we can attempt to have representatives from all the Orthodox Churches resume discussing the topic of Autocephaly amongst themselves. They can decide how autocephaly is to be granted and how a Tome of Autocephaly should be signed. The discussion between the representatives of the Churches should be based on the many texts which were prepared during the numerous, arduous, pre-conciliar conferences. These texts were meant to be presented at the Great and Holy Council of Crete, but unfortunately that never happened. Once the representatives' efforts are successful and an agreement is reached, a pan-Orthodox Council should be convened to review the Ukrainian issue on the basis of the new information and in accordance with the sacred canons and the timeless practice of the Orthodox Church. Once the council ratifies the agreements, the Ukrainian ecclesiastical question will be permanently resolved. I firmly believe that pan-Orthodox consultation is the only way to successfully resolve the long-standing Ukrainian issue and, consequently, to overcome the present crisis which threatens the unity of the Orthodox Church with schism. In the face of the current catastrophic impasse, we cannot remain idle, detached, apathetic, and indifferent. We must all feel a sense of duty and urgency, and all the Orthodox Churches everywhere should take the initiative to bring about a brotherly pan-Orthodox consultation in order to resolve the Ukrainian issue.

I am convinced that dialogue is the only way out of the present impasse. We must avoid repeating the tragedy of 1054, and we must prevent Orthodoxy from experiencing the greatest schism in its history. Dialogue is the only antidote to the irrationality of the egotistical lust for glory which undermines Orthodox unity. Dialogue is the only way to overcome our selfish obsessions and achieve ecclesiastical unity and peace. Today, when inter-Christian and inter-religious dialogues are so prevalent, we cannot refuse to engage in inter-Orthodox dialogue. We cannot refuse to consult with our fellow bishops and brother primates of the Autocephalous Orthodox Churches. The learned Metropolitan Nicholas of Mesogeia asks, "How is it justifiable for our ecclesiastical leaders to loudly support inter-Christian and inter-religious dialogue and yet reject communication amongst themselves?"[133]

On November 30, 2019, during a patriarchal concelebration with Patriarch Theodoros II of Alexandria, Ecumenical

Patriarch Bartholomew addressed a delegation from the Vatican, led by Cardinal Koch. Patriarch Bartholomew expressed his satisfaction with the Joint International Commission for Theological Dialogue between the Catholic Church and the Eastern Orthodox Church, and the progress it made on the two critical issues of Primacy and Conciliarity in the second millennium. He spoke of "the dialogue of love and truth between the Orthodox and Roman Catholic Churches that has been ongoing since 1964."[134] And yet the same Patriarch Bartholomew has definitively closed the door of dialogue and stubbornly refuses a pan-Orthodox consultation with his brothers in Christ, the primates of the other Orthodox Churches, to find a solution to the ecclesiastical crisis which threatens the Orthodox Church with schism. Unfortunately, instead of this, there is a theory developing within the circles of the Ecumenical Patriarchate that "the Ecumenical Patriarchate took the first step. Two other Churches followed. In practice, since the issuing of the Tome, the whole issue has already been given over to pan-Orthodox consultation ... in these cases the path is a one-way street, and recognition will come in due course,"[135] while others add that the present crisis is "a dust-cloud which will pass."

In response to this theory, we say that without dialogue the problem will not be resolved; on the contrar, it will grow and threaten to drown us. The first fissures in the Body of the Church are already evident after Greece and Alexandria's hasty and largely incomprehensible recognition of Ukraine's pseudo-autocephaly. If a dialogue of love between all the Orthodox Churches does not begin immediately, these fissures will become a great and painful schism which will forever damage the Orthodox Church. Therefore, it is our collective responsibility as Orthodox bishops to preserve unity, according to the Lord's commandment: "Holy Father, keep through Your name those whom You have given Me, that they may be one as We are" (John 17:11).

Epilogue

The present study is the result of my anguish and suffering over the unity of Orthodoxy, a unity which is currently being undermined by this painful crisis which threatens to divide the Orthodox Church. As I conclude, I feel the need to once more stress that I stand in awe of, and have the greatest respect for, the Ecumenical Patriarchate and its leadership, the leadership of the First Throne of Orthodoxy, the Church of Constantinople, whose glory echoes through the ages. We do not in any way dispute that the pulse of Orthodoxy has always beat in Constantinople, that city adorned by the sacred palladium of Orthodoxy and the Greek nation, the renowned temple of the Holy Wisdom of God, which, "for reasons only the Lord knows," is today desecrated by its non-Orthodox captors.

In the Constantinople of legend and Greek sighs, in this all holy center of Orthodoxy, "Ecumenical Councils were convened, doctrinal definitions were articulated, liturgical traditions were shaped, saints and confessors were recognized, and the All-Holy Mother of God," the Champion Leader of our nation, "was honored."[136]

In Constantinople, the immortal see of the Ecumenical Patriarchate, the ecclesiastical arts "which critically influenced a very large part of the world, from the depths of Russia to the mountains of Armenia and from Sicily to the desert of Sinai"[137] were cultivated.

It was in Constantinople, in the Holy and Great Church of Christ, that the authentic formulation of the Christian message in the historical life of the Church was put forth.

In short, as Greek Orthodox Christians, we will always honor and revere the Ecumenical Patriarchate of Constantinople, the Patriarchate of our Greek nation. However, our reverence and love for it does not give us the right to turn a blind eye to its authoritarian, uncanonical, and unacceptable ecclesiological actions. There is no doubt that the Ecumenical Patriarchate's unilateral decision to grant autocephaly to Ukraine creates a serious problem that threatens pan-Orthodox unity, and we cannot willingly accept that. Moreover, the Patriarchate of Constantinople's claim that it can assume the role of pan-Orthodox authority on major ecclesiastical, dogmatic, or canonical issues is unsubstantiated, and is not in keeping with canonical tradition and historical ecclesiastical order and practice. The Ecumenical Patriarchate's attempt to misinterpret "privileges of honor," transforming them into a "primacy of authority" warps Orthodox ecclesiology and conspires against the Conciliarity of the Church. For "the organization of the Orthodox Church is based on conciliarity, not on an isolated, absolutized Primate, something which reveals the temptation of Popery."[138]

Faced with the danger of the alteration of Orthodox ecclesiology, Orthodox hierarchs must remember the sacred oaths we made before God and men during our ordination to the Episcopate: that we would keep the sacred canons and preserve the unity of the Orthodox Church throughout the world. We must therefore fearlessly, boldly, and courageously work to preserve the sacred Canons and the Conciliar, Hierarchical System of the Orthodox Church.

Today, as we all live through the dangerous, divisive crisis surrounding the Ukrainian issue, I could not remain cold and indifferent in the face of the tragic division which threatens to tear apart the Body of the One, Holy, Catholic, and Apostolic Church. Schism is at the gates, after Alexandria and Greece followed in the footsteps of Constantinople, accepting the Eumenical Patriarch's unilateral decision regarding Ukrainian autocephaly, and my hierarchal conscience does not allow me to silently accept the tragic obstinacy and catastrophic mistakes which will permanently divide global Orthodoxy. Therefore, not entangled by the web of nationalism, and inspired by the Apostle Peter's declaration following Pentecost, "We ought to obey God rather than men" (Acts 5:29), I will modestly, but courageously, proclaim the truth always and everywhere, without fearing consequences from the religious or political powers that be.

After all, we have the eternal example of the Church's Founder, the God-Man and our Redeemer, Christ, who came to earth to proclaim the truth, without fearing the consequences from the rulers of the age, the kings and high priests, declaring that " ... I have come into the world, that I should bear witness to the truth. Everyone who is of the truth hears My voice" (John 18:37). To quote a passage which perfectly reflects my own feelings, I am certain that "Many ethnophyletic critics will accuse us of an anti-patriotic and anti-Hellenic attitude. I will not contradict the ancient Greek saying, 'Plato is a friend, but the truth is a better friend', nor our national poet Dionysios Solomos, who says 'We must regard as "national" that which is true.' I am much more inclined to the position that we Christians must place above our earthly homelands our heavenly homeland and its presence on earth, the Church, of which we are all members and citizens regardless of race or nationality—Greeks, Russians, Serbs, Bulgarians, Georgians, Romanians, Arabs. We are all members of the one Body of Christ, which is the Church, and in Christ 'there is neither Jew nor Greek, there is neither slave nor free, there is neither male nor female; for you are all one in Christ Jesus' (Galatians 3:28)."[139]

For me, least amongst bishops, faith in the Triune God and His All-Immaculate Church, and reverence for the divine and sacred canons and the timeless tradition of the Orthodox faith is above everyone and everything. This is why I will be outspoken in defending the faith, and the strict observance of canonical traditions and ecclesiastical institutions. My battle is inspired by the shining example of one whose sandals I am not worthy to tie, the fiery champion of Orthodoxy, Mark Eugenikos. During the critical and terrible days of the Council of Ferrara-Florence (1438–39), he fought, tirelessly and resiliently, until the end. With a pure Orthodox *phronema [mindset or outlook]*, he struggled for the Orthodox faith, alone against everyone. So, the paean, centuries earlier attributed to Athanasius the Great, can be also said of him. He was "the most heroic saint and the saintliest hero."[140]

His bold reply to the emperor, "I will not do this, no matter what happens", and his proclamation, "No concession may be made in matters of the faith"[141] have made him the sacred symbol of the fighting hierarch, and anyone who struggles for the Christian faith.

Standing with Saint Mark Eugenikos, with a heart full of anguish, I cry out and declare: "No concession may be made in matters concerning the divine and sacred Canons." As a hierarch of the Orthodox Church, burning with the flame of sincere love for the unity of the faith, I will always fight, without hesitation, to preserve the sacred canonical tradition of the One, Holy, Catholic and Apostolic Church, and ensure that her unity is safeguarded.

Today, the whole world around and within us is constantly being overturned and transformed.

Today, an era of globalizing power is eliminating borders and homogenizing humankind, not only in terms of nations, but in terms of religion.

Today, in these critical and world-changing times, as the winds of rejection blow stronger and stormier around us, all bishops of the Orthodox Church, and especially her leaders, the primates of all the Orthodox Churches, should not become emissaries of fracture and division, but rather apostles of love, humility, and, above all, unity. The unity of Christ's Church is the highest good. It is so very envied by the devil and also so very threatened by human weakness and sin.

Today, the explosive development of technology does away with God and deifies man.

Today, technological civilization madly demolishes every spiritual aptitude and every metaphysical concern.

Today, humans are not interested in eternity, because they do not believe in it, only caring about their earthly well-being, pleasure, and honor.

In this faithless, demonic, and Christ-denying age, which does not hesitate to persecute the Church, a bishop cannot be considered worthy of his mission if he is not unceasingly anxious over the divisive situation which global Orthodoxy is currently experiencing. Orthodox bishops all need to engage in dialogue with one another in love. We need to strive to secure the Church's unity, and, with mutual understanding and solidarity, strengthen her voice in the events of our time, so that she may once again be in a position to give the world a new witness to the Lord's Cross and Resurrection. In this way, we may help today's faithless masses know that Christ, by His sacrifice on the Cross and life-giving Resurrection, redeemed humankind from the miserable weight of death, and reopened the gate of eternity and immortality that sin had closed. It is just as imperative today as it has been in every era that our Church be united, so that it may have the ability, drive, and vigor to guard the deposit of Evangelical Truth, and to keep pure and immaculate that which she received from the Lord, and for which the apostles, prophets, martyrs, saints and hierarchs fought the good fight.

We could have concluded here, but as the writing of the present study was coming to an end, the blustering neo-sultan of Ankara, the fanatical islamist president of Turkey, Recep Tayyip Erdoğan, who dreams of restoring the Ottoman Empire, determined to revise the status of that monument of unique architectural interest and global civilizational heritage, the sacred temple of the Holy Wisdom of God in Constantinople. It was with heartfelt anguish that I was informed that he was reverting it into a mosque for the worship needs of the Muslim community. This outrageous abomination took place despite the intense, albeit non-collective, reactions of primates and hierarchs of Orthodox Churches, spiritual leaders of various denominations and other religions, numerous international organizations, and political leaders of several countries. I could not, however, overlook the fact that one of the first Orthodox Churches to directly and vigorously react to the president of Turkey's abominable crime was the Orthodox Church of Russia.

Despite the bitterness and frustration that they feel on account of the anti-canonical grant of "Autocephaly" to schismatic ecclesiastical groups in Ukraine, both the primate of the Russian Church, Patriarch Kirill, and the Holy Patriarchal Synod of Russia wrote immediate statements strenuously and harshly decrying the abhorrent actions of the Turkish authorities. Transforming the Sacred Church of Hagia Sophia, this masterpiece of the Christian spirit, which for about a thousand years had functioned as an Orthodox Christian church, into a mosque, was publicly condemned. In the communiqué immediately following its July 16–17, 2020 session, the Holy Synod of the Orthodox Church of Russia expressed its deep sorrow over Turkey's decision to remove the Church of Hagia Sophia's museum status, and give it over to the Muslim community for use in worship, stressing that:

> Hagia Sophia was built in honor of Christ the Saviour, remaining a church in the consciousness of millions of Christians. And to

the Orthodox Church this cathedral is of special historical and spiritual importance. Addressing our fellow Orthodox Churches everywhere, we note with great sadness that this dismal event has found the Orthodox world divided, as a direct consequence of the uncanonical legalization of the schism in Ukraine, which weakened our ability to come together to oppose new spiritual threats and civilizational challenges. Now, at a time of growing Christianophobia and increasing pressure on the Church from the secular society, unity is needed more than ever. We call upon our fellow Orthodox Churches everywhere to work together in the spirit of peace and love in Christ in order to seek ways to overcome the crisis. We hope that the Turkish authorities will take necessary steps to preserve the priceless Christian mosaics which have miraculously survived to this day and will ensure access to them for Christian pilgrims … we also call upon the world community to render all possible assistance in any way possible in maintaining the special status of Hagia Sophia, which is of timeless importance to all Christians.[142]

Later, a few days before Hagia Sophia's conversion into a mosque, Patriarch Kirill of Moscow and All Russia expressed his own deep concern over certain Turkish politicians' appeals to change the status of the Church of Hagia Sophia, one of the greatest masterpieces of Christian and global civilization. In a written statement, he noted the following beautiful and incredible sentiments:

Built in the 6th century in honor of Christ the Saviour, this church is of great importance to all of Orthodoxy. And it is especially dear to the Russian Church. Prince Vladimir's envoys stepped across the threshold of this church and were captivated by its heavenly beauty. Having heard their story, St. Vladimir decided to be baptized, and baptize the entire Russian peoples, who followed him into a new spiritual and historical dimension: Christian civilization.

Through many generations, we have inherited an admiration for the achievements of this civilization, of which we were not a part, and Hagia Sophia has always been one of its devoutly venerated symbols. The image of this church has become deeply ingrained in our culture and history, having given strength and inspiration to our great architects in Kiev, Novgorod, Polotsk, and all the major centers of spiritual formation in Early Russia …

In the long history of the relations between Rus and Constantinople, there have been many different stages, and sometimes some difficult periods. But, like before, so now, the Russian people responded and respond with bitterness and indignation to any attempt to degrade or trample upon the millennium-old spiritual heritage of the Church of Constantinople. A threat to Hagia Sophia is a threat to the entire Christian civilization and, therefore, to our spirituality and history. To this day Hagia Sophia remains a great Christian shrine for every Russian Orthodox believer.

It is a duty of every civilized state to maintain balance, and to reconcile society rather than aggravate discords in it. They must help unite people, not divide them.

Today the relationship between Turkey and Russia is developing dynamically, but one should keep in mind that Russia is an Orthodox-majority country so, what may happen to Hagia Sophia is of great and emotional concern to the Russian people.

I hope for prudence in Turkey's state leadership. Preservation of the current neutral status of Hagia Sophia, one of the greatest masterpieces of Christian culture and an ecclesiastical symbol for millions of Christians all over the world, will … help strengthen any continuing interfaith peace and accord."[143]

The Orthodox Church of Russia demonstrated and held an assertive stance when dealing with the issue of transforming the Church of the Holy Wisdom of God into a mosque. Seeing this, all the Orthodox Churches throughout the world should, in a spirit of peace, truth, and Christlike love, lend a receptive ear to the anguished cry of the Holy Synod and primate of the Russian Church, who seek to find a way out of the impasse created by the Ecumenical Patriarchate's anti-canonical grant of "Autocephaly" to non-canonical schismatic groups in Ukraine. This can only be done by initiating an inter-Orthodox dialogue, which will help overcome the crisis and consolidate unity, thus avoiding a catastrophic schism in the Church. Today, in a world which is spiritually confused, which is suffering a crisis of values, and which is questioning everything, the Orthodox Church must restore her unity and proceed to reorganize her spiritual powers to meet modern challenges. Only through forging unity will the Orthodox Church be in a position to deal successfully with contemporary problems and defend the Orthodox faith effectively. Only in this way will the Orthodox

Church be in a position to effectively participate in spiritual dialogue, to face the problems of our age, and to bear witness to the Orthodox faith and life in the historical development of the world.

I pray that Christ our Redeemer, the Crucified and Risen God-Man, "with the temptation will also make the way of escape" (1 Corinthians 10:13). I pray that He may give prudence and enlightenment to all, and especially to the primates, the leaders of Orthodoxy, that without hegemonic tendencies and authoritarian dispositions they may offer our Church a dialogue of brotherly love, the fragrant witness of unity.

Notes

1   "Χρησιμοποιούμεναι ξενόγλωσσοι φράσεις (ἐκ τῆς Λατινικῆς καί ἄλλων γλωσσῶν)," Νεώτερον Ἐγκυκλοπαιδικόν Λεξικόν Ἡλίου, τόμος 18ος [Phrases used in other languages, New Encyclopedic Lexicon Sun, volume 18] (Athens, n.d.), 1053.

2   See the Divine Liturgy of Our Father among the Saints John Chrysostom: Slavonic-English Parallel Text 4th edition (Jordanville, New York: Holy Trinity Publications, 2015) p.141.

3   Π. Β. ΠΑΣΧΟΥ, Ὁ διάλογος μέ τή Δύση γιά τό Θεό καί τόν ἄνθρωπο - Ἡ ποιητική θεολογία τοῦ Pavel Nicolaievitch Evdokimov [P. V. Paschos. Dialogue with the West Concerning God and Man: The Poetic Theology of Pavel Nicolaievitch Evdokimov] (Athens, 1995), 9.

4   This is an allusion to the Exapostilarion (hymn) of Christmas: "We, who were in darkness and shadow have found the Truth." See also Matthew 4:16.

5   2 Corinthians 2:17.

6   ΧΡ. Ν. ΠΑΠΟΥΤΣΟΠΟΥΛΟΥ (Ἀρχιμ.), Λόγοι τῆς Χάριτος, [Hr. N. Papoutsopoulos, Words of Grace] (Athens, 1969), 31.

7   Γ. Β. ΜΕΛΕΤΗ, Διάλογος μέ τόν οὐρανό [G. V. Meletis, Dialogue with Heaven] (Athens, 1974), 174.

8   1 Peter 4:14.

9   Matthew 5:11.

10 Psalm 23:4.

11 Romans 1:8.

12 Γ. Α. ΡΑΛΛΗ - Μ. ΠΟΤΛΗ, Σύνταγμα τῶν Θείων καί Ἱερῶν Κανόνων τῶν τε Ἁγίων καί Πανευφήμων Ἀποστόλων, καί τῶν Ἱερῶν Οἰκουμενικῶν καί Τοπικῶν Συνόδων, καί τῶν κατά μέρος Ἁγίων Πατέρων, τόμος Β΄ [G.A. Rallis, M. Potlis, Constitution of the Divine and Holy Canons of the Holy and Disciples, and the Holy Ecumenical and Local Councils. Vol. 2] (Athens, 1852), 173. Canon 3 of the Second Ecumenical Council in Constantinople states that "The

Bishop of Constantinople ... shall have the prerogative of honor after the Bishop of Rome; because Constantinople is New Rome," 281. Canon 28 of the Fourth Ecumenical Council in Chalcedon: "We ourselves have also decreed and voted the same things about the prerogatives of the very holy church of this same Constantinople, New Rome. The Fathers in fact have correctly attributed the prerogatives (which belong) to the see of the most ancient Rome because it was the imperial city. And thus, moved by the same reasoning, the one hundred and fifty bishops (*sic*, the actual number was 650) beloved of God have accorded equal prerogatives to the very holy see of New Rome, justly considering that the city that is honored by the imperial power and the senate and enjoying (within the civil order) the prerogatives equal to those of Rome, the most ancient imperial city, ought to be as elevated as Old Rome in the affairs of the Church, being in the second place after it."

13   The Second Ecumenical Council in Constantinople in 381, the Fifth Ecumenical Council in Constantinople in 553, the Sixth Ecumenical Council in 680, and the Quinsext Council in Trullo in 691.

14   The First Ecumenical Council in Nicaea of Bithynia in 325, the Third Ecumenical Council in Ephesus in 431, the Fourth Ecumenical Council in Chalcedon in 451, and the Seventh Ecumenical Council in Nicaea in 787.

15   Translator's note: Βασιλεύουσα, (Vasilevousa), a name for Constantinople which originated in Late Antiquity.

16   ΒΛ. ΙΩ. ΦΕΙΔΑ, «Τό Οἰκουμενικό Πατριαρχεῖο. Ἡ διαχρονική ἐκκλησιαστική διακονία του» in *Τό Οἰκουμενικό Πατριαρχεῖο - Ἡ Μεγάλη τοῦ Χριστοῦ Ἐκκλησία* [*Vl. Io. Fidas, The Ecumenical Patriarchate, Its Ecclesiastical Ministry through the Ages, in The Ecumenical Patriarchate: Christ's Great Church*] (Athens, 1989), 30.

17   Ibid., 31.

18   Ibid., 11.

19   John Chrysostom, *Homily XI, On the Epistle to the Ephesians*, P.G. 62, 85.

20   Γ. ΘΕΟΤΟΚΑ, Ἡ Ὀρθοδοξία στόν καιρό μας—Δοκίμια [G. Theotokas, *Orthodoxy in Our Time—Essays*] (Athens, 1975), 44.

21   See the 9th Ekos of the Akathist hymn: "We see most eloquent orators mute as fish before Thee, O Theotokos." Prayer Book (Jordanville, New York: Holy Trinity Publications, 2005), p.305.

22 The Great Endemic Synod was a permanent standing synod of the church of Constantinople, presided over by the patriarch.

23 The four patriarchates of the East are Constantinople, Alexandria, Antioch, and Jerusalem.

24 Θ. Ν. ΖΗΣΗ, *Τό Οὐκρανικό Αὐτοκέφαλο* [Protopresbyter Th. Zisis, *The Autocephaly of Ukraine*] (Thessaloniki, 2019), 90.

25 Translator's note: Επιτροπικως. Epitropikos. "In guardianship," or "in trust." Meaning to act as custodian or executor, while Constantinople retains overall authority.

26 «Αὐτοκεφαλία τῆς Ἐκκλησίας τῆς Οὐκρανίας. Εἰσήγησις τοῦ Μακαριωτάτου Ἀρχιεπισκόπου Ἀθηνῶν καί πάσης Ἑλλάδος Ἱερωνύμου», *Ἐκκλησία*, τόμος 96ος [*The Autocephaly of the Church of Ukraine, an Opinion by His Eminence Archbishop Ieronymos of Athens and All Greece*] (October 2019), 854.

27 «Ἐπιστολή Μητροπολίτη Βιδυνίου Δανιήλ στούς Ἱεράρχες τῶν Ἐκκλησιῶν γιά τό Οὐκρανικό» [*Letter from Metropolitan Daniel of Vidin to the Hierarchs of the Church Regarding the Ukrainian Issue*] June 19, 2019, https://spzh.news/gr/zashhita-very/62935-obrashhenije-mitropolita-vidin skogo-ijerarkham -cerkvej-po-ukrainskoj-probleme. English version: https://spzh.news/en/zashhita-very/62935-obrashhenije-mitropolita-vi%20dinskogo-ijerarkham-cerkvej-po-ukrainskoj-probleme [Translator's note: Nikiforos quotes the Greek version of Daniel of Vidin's letter somewhat differently. The original Greek text is as following: "*καί ἡ Μητρόπολις αὕτη Κιόβου ἔστω ὑποκειμένη ὑπό τον Ἁγιώτατον Πατριαρχικόν τῆς Μοσχοβίας θρόνον, καί οι εν αὐτῇ ἀρχιερατεύοντες, ὅι τε ἤδη καί οἱ μετά τούτον, γινώσκωσι γέροντα καί προεστῶτα αὐτόν τον κατά καιρούς Πατριάρχην Μοσχοβίας ὡς υπ αὐτοῦ χειροτονούμενοι*", which translates as "and this Metropolis of Kiev be subject to the Most Holy Patriarchal Throne of Muscovy, and both its current and future bishops must know that their senior and head is whoever over the years is Patriarch of Muscovy, as they are consecrated by him".] The original text of this letter, along with the contemporary official Russian translation and a modern Russian translation can be found in: B. N. Floria et al., *Vossoedinie Kievskoi Mitropolii c Russkoi Pravoslavnoi Tserov'iu 1676-1686 gg. Issledovaniia i dokumenty* (Moscow: Tserkovno-nauchnyi tsentr "Pravoslavnaia entsiklopediia," 2019), 695–705.]

28 ΒΛ. ΙΩ. ΦΕΙΔΑ, «Τό "Αὐτοκέφαλον" καί τό "Αὐτόνομον" ἐν τῇ Ὀρθοδόξῳ Ἐκκλησίᾳ», *Νέα Σιών*, ἔτος οα΄, τεῦχος Α΄ [V. Fidas. *"Autocephaly" and*

"*Autonomy*" *in the Orthodox Church.* New Zion, year 71] (January–June 1979), 16.

29   *Letter from Metropolitan Daniel of Vidin.* 2019.

30   ΑΝ. Κ. ΓΚΟΤΣΟΠΟΥΛΟΥ, «Μικρή συμβολή στόν διάλογο γιά τό Οὐκρανικό Ἀὐτοκέφαλο'"», [Protopresbyter Anastasios Gotsopoulos, *A small contribution to the discussion concerning Ukrainian autocephaly*] Jan. 8, 2019, *https://www.impantokratoros.gr/961E0E58.el.aspx˙* See also "Σύγκληση Πανορθόδοξης Συνόδου γιά τό Οὐκρανικό ζητοῦν 4 Μητροπολίτες (Κονίτσης Ἀνδρέας, Πειραιῶς Σεραφείμ, Κηθύρων Σεραφείμ καί Αἰτωλίας Κοσμᾶς)», [*Four Metropolitans, Andreas of Konitsa, Serafeim of Pereus, Serafim of Kithira, and Kosmas of Etolia, Request the Convocation of a Panorthodox Synod regarding the Ukrainian issue*] November 29, 2019, *www. ethnos.gr/ekklisia/ekklisia-tis-ellados/74798_sygklisi-panorthodoxis -synodoy- gia-oykraniko-zitoyn-4*

31   Gotsopoulos, *A Small Contribution,* 2019.

32   Fidas, *The Ecumenical Patriarchate,* 34.

33   A reference to the Widow's Mite in Mark 12:41–44, Luke 21:1–4.

34   ΒΑΡΘΟΛΟΜΑΙΟΥ, «Πρός τόν Οὐκρανικόν λαόν (26 Ἰουλίου 2008)», Ὀρθοδοξία, περίοδος Βʹ, ἔτος ΙΕʹ, τεῦχος Γʹ [Bartholomew, Archbishop of Constantinople and Ecumenical Patriarch *To the Ukrainian People*] in *Orthodoxy* magazine, per. 2, year 15. Vol. 3] (July–September 2008), 532–3 [English: https://www.archons.org/-/ecumenical-patriarch-bartholomew-delivers-speech-to-the-ukrainian-nation-during-1020th-baptismal-anniversary-of-kiev-russia].

35   ΑΝ. Γ. ΓΚΟΤΣΟΠΟΥΛΟΥ, «Ἀπλές ἐρωτήσεις κατανόησις κειμένου Βʹ» [Anastasios Gotsopoulos, *Simple Questions for Understanding Passage 2*] August 22, 2019, *https://www.romfea.gr/epi kairotita-xronika/31070-aples-erotiseis-katanoisis-keimenou-b*

36   Ibid.

37   Archbishop Ieronymos, *The Autocephaly of the Church of Ukraine,* 855.

38   Κ. ΔΕΛΙΚΑΝΗ, *Τά ἐν τοῖς κώδιξι τοῦ Πατριαρχικοῦ Ἀρχειοφυλακίου σωζόμενα ἐπίσημα ἐκκλησιαστικά ἔγγραφα, τά ἀφορῶντα εἰς τάς σχέσεις τοῦ Οἰκουμενικοῦ Πατριαρχείου πρός τάς Ἐκκλησίας Ρωσσίας, Βλαχίας καί Μολδαβίας, Σερβίας, Ἀχριδῶν καί Πεκίου 1564-1863, τόμος Γʹ* [*Formal Ecclesiastical Documents Concerning the Relationship of the Ecumenical Patriarchate with the Churches of Russia, Vlahia and Moldavia, Serbia, Ohrid, and Pekio, in the codices of, and*

preserved in the Archives of the Ecumenical Patriarchate] (Constantinople, 1905), 36.

39 Ibid. 34.

40 Θ. Ν. ΖΗΣΗ, *Κωνσταντινούπολη καί Μόσχα* [Protopresbyter Theodore Zisis, *Constantinople and Moscow*] (Thessaloniki, 1989), 31.

41 Β. Κ. ΣΤΕΦΑΝΙΔΟΥ, *Ἐκκλησιαστική Ἱστορία, ἀπ' ἀρχῆς μέχρι σήμερον* [Archimandrite V. Stefanidis, *Ecclesiastical History, from the Beginning* to Today] (Athens,1959), 448.

42 Β. Δ. ΤΖΩΡΤΖΑΤΟΥ, *Οἱ βασικοί θεσμοί διοικήσεως τῶν Ὀρθοδόξων Πατριαρχείων, μετά ἱστορικῶν ἀνασκοπήσεων* [V. D Georgatos, Metropolitan of Kitros, *The Basic Rules of Governance of the Orthodox Patriachates, with a Historical Overview*] (Athens, 1972), 169.

43 ΒΛ. ΙΩ. ΦΕΙΔΑ, *Ἐκκλησιαστική Ἱστορία τῆς Ρωσίας (988-1988)* [V. Fidas, *Ecclesiastical History of Russia*] (Athens, 1988), 273–4.

44 Ibid., 301–4.

45 Ibid., 317–19.

46 Ibid., 335–6.

47 Ibid., 348–9. Also see Georgatos, *The Basic Rules*, 177.

48 ΒΛ. ΙΩ. ΦΕΙΔΑ, «Ἡ Συνοδική Πράξη τοῦ Οἰκουμενικοῦ Πατριαρχείου (1686) καί ἡ Αὐτοκεφαλία τῆς Ἐκκλησίας Οὐκρανίας» [Fidas, *The Synodical Act of the Ecumenical Patriarchate (1686), and the Autocephaly of the Church of Ukraine*] November 28, 2018, *https://orthodoxia.info/news/h -συνοδική-πράξη-του-οικουμενικού-πατρ/*

49 E.M Polygenis, *Kallistos of Diokleia: I Don't Agree with the Phanar, but I also Don't Agree with Moscow* (December 14, 2018. A video of this interview can be found here: https://youtu.be/hFmJe50cbeg).

50 Ibid.

51 Ibid.

52 Daniel of Vidin, *Letter to the Hierarchs.* 2019.

53 ΑΓΑΠΙΟΥ ΙΕΡΟΜΟΝΑΧΟΥ ΚΑΙ ΝΙΚΟΔΗΜΟΥ ΜΟΝΑΧΟΥ, *Πηδάλιον,* [Nikodimos the Hagiorite and Hieromonk Agapios, *The Rudder*] (Athens, 1957), 199.

54 Ibid., 240.

55 Rallis, Potlis, *Constitution of the Divine and Holy Canons. Vol.2,* 169.

56 Ibid., 203.

57 Ibid., 216–17.

58   Ibid., 309–10.

59   Ibid., 556. See also Π. Ι. ΜΠΟΥΜΗ, Ἡ ἀκρίβεια καί ἡ ἀλήθεια τῶν Ἱερῶν
       Κανόνων (Ἐπιστασία - ἑρμηνευτικόν γύμνασμα ἐπί τῶν 91ου καί 92ου Κανόνων
       τοῦ Μ. Βασιλείου) [P.I Boumis, Professor at the University of Athens, *The
       Exactness and the Truth of the Holy Canons*] (Katerini, 1996), 145.

60   Α. Σ. ΑΛΙΒΙΖΑΤΟΥ, Οἱ Ἱεροί Κανόνες και οἱ Ἐκκλησιαστικοί Νόμοι [A.S.
       Alivizatos, *The Holy Canons and the Ecclesiastical Regulations*] (Athens,
       1949), 19.

61   Ibid., 21.

62   Δ. ΙΩ. ΚΩΝΣΤΑΝΤΕΛΟΥ, Ἐθνική ταυτότητα καί Θρησκευτική
       ἰδιαιτερότητα τοῦ Ἑλληνισμοῦ, [Protopresbyter D. J. Konstantelos, *The
       National Identity and the Religious Uniqueness of Hellenism*] (Athens, 1993),
       197.

63   «Δήλωση τῆς Ἱερᾶς Συνόδου τῆς Ὀρθοδόξου Ἐκκλησίας τῆς Ρωσίας γιά τήν
       παράνομη εἰσπήδηση τοῦ Πατριαρχείου Κωνσταντινουπόλεως στό κανονικό
       ἔδαφος τῆς Ὀρθοδόξου Ἐκκλησίας τῆς Ρωσίας», [Statement of the Holy
       Synod of the Orthodox Church of Russia Regarding the Patriarchate of
       Constantinople's Illegal Encroachment into the Canonical Territory of the
       Orthodox Church of Russia] September 14, 2018, *http://www.patriarchia.
       ru/gr/db/text/5268288.html* [English: http://www.patriarchia.ru/en/db/
       text/5268290.html].

64   Βλ. τά σχετικά στήν Ἐπιστολή, μέ ἀρ. πρωτ. 532, τοῦ Ἀρχιεπισκόπου
       Κωνσταντινουπόλεως καί Οἰκουμενικοῦ Πατριάρχη Ἀθηναγόρα πρός τόν
       Πατριάρχη Σόφιας καί πάσης Βουλγαρίας Κύριλλο, «ἐξαγγελτήριον τῆς
       ἀναγνωρίσεως τῆς γενομένης πράξεως περί ἀνυψώσεως εἰς τήν πατριαρχικήν
       ἀξίαν τῆς ἐν Βουλγαρίᾳ Ὀρθοδόξου Ἐκκλησίας», στό περιοδικό Ὀρθοδοξία
       36 [Letter from Archbishop of Constantinople and Ecumenical Patriarch
       Athenagoras to the Patriarch of Sofia and All Bulgaria, Cyril. *Announcement
       of the Elevation of the Orthodox Church of Bulgaria to a Patriarchate.*
       Orthodoxy Magazine, 36] (1961), 303–4.

65   See Gotsopoulos, *A Small Contribution.* 2019. https://mospat.ru/
       gr/2019/03/15/news171593/[https://gr.pravoslavie.ru/127793.html].

66   Fidas, *Autocephaly and Autonomy,* 23.

67   Β. ΣΤΑΥΡΙΔΟΥ, Συνοπτική Ἱστορία τοῦ Οἰκουμενικοῦ Πατριαρχείου, [V.
       Stavridis, *A Synoptic History of the Ecumenical* Patriarchate] (Thessaloniki,
       1991), 70.

68 «Δήλωση τῆς Ἱερᾶς Συνόδου τῆς Ὀρθοδόξου Ἐκκλησίας τῆς Ρωσίας», [Statement of the Holy Synod of the Orthodox Church of Russia] October 17, 2019, *https://mospat.ru/gr/2019/10/17/news178948/*[English: https://mospat.ru/en/news/46006/].

69 Ibid.

70 "*Four* Metropolitans ... Request" 2019.

71 Σ. ΣΟΥΜΙΛΟ, «Ἕνα παλαιό πρόβλημα τῆς νέας Ἐκκλησίας. Τό Κίνημα τοῦ Λιπκόφσκι ὡς πνευματικό, κανονικό καί ἐκκλησιολογικό πρόβλημα τῶν ἐν Οὐκρανίᾳ Ἐκκλησιῶν» [S. Soumilo, President of the International Institute of the Athonite Legacy in Kiev, "An Old Problem of the New Church: The Lypkivsky Movement as a Spiritual, Canonical, and Ecclesiological Problem of the Churches in Ukraine"] June 2, 2020, *https://www.romfea. gr/katigories/10 -apopseis/29502-ena-palaio-problima-tis-neas-ekklisias*

72 Nikodimos, *Rudder*, 206.

73 Nikodimos, *Rudder*, 538–9. See also, «Ἡ ἀπό πάσης τῆς ἐν Ἀφρικῇ Συνόδου, πρός Βονιφάτιον τόν τῆς Ρωμαίων Ἐκκλησίας Ἐπίσκοπον, διά Φαυστίνου Ἐπισκόπου, Φιλίππου καί Ἀσέλλου πρεσβυτέρου, τῶν τοποτηρητῶν τῆς Ρωμαϊκῆς Ἐκκλησίας, ἀποσταλεῖσα Ἐπιστολή Α΄». [First Letter from the Entire African Synod to Boniface, Bishop of the Church of Rome. Sent through Faustinus, Bishop of Filppi, and the Priest Asellos, Serving as Representatives of the Roman Church].

74 Nikodimos, *Rudder*, 540–2: See Also, «Ἐπιστολή Β΄ τῆς ἐν Ἀφρικῇ Συνόδου πρός Κελεστῖνον τόν Πάπαν». [Second Letter of the African Synod: to Pope Celestine].

75 Nikodimos, *Rudder*, 541.

76 Ibid., 542.

77 Ibid., 482.

78 Ibid., 535.

79 Ibid., 206.

80 Ibid., 191; canon 9, 199; canon 17.

81 Ibid., 192.

82 bid., 193.

83 ΣΕΡΑΦΕΙΜ, «Ποτέ δέν ἀποδέχθηκα πρόταση γιά ἀναγνώριση τῆς ἀνυπόστατης "Ἐκκλησίας" πού δημιουργήθηκε στήν Οὐκρανία» [Metropolitan Serafim of Pireas, "I Never Accepted a Proposal to Recognize the Non-Existent Church Which Was Created in Ukraine],

October.   13,   2019,   *https://www.romfea.gr/epikairotita-xronika/32274-peiraios-po*   *te-den-apodexthika-protasi-gia-anagnorisi-tis-anupostatis-ekklisias-pou-dimiourgithike-stin-oukrania*

84   *"Four* Metropolitans Request ..." 2019. See also. Π. Ι. ΠΑΝΑΓΙΩΤΑΚΟΥ, *Σύστημα τοῦ Ἐκκλησιαστικοῦ Δικαίου κατά τήν ἐν Ἑλλάδι ἰσχύν αὐτοῦ, τόμος Γ΄, Τό Ποινικόν Δίκαιον τῆς Ἐκκλησίας,* [P. I Panagiotakos, *The System of Ecclesiastical Jurisprudence in Greece,* in Vol. 3 of *Legislation of the Church*] (Athens, 1962), 836–8.

85   *Καταστατικός Χάρτης τῆς Ἁγιωτάτης Ἐκκλησίας τῆς Κύπρου,* [Article 81 of the Constitutional Charter of the Most Holy Church of Cyprus] (Lefkosia, 2010), 53.

86   Nikodimos, *Rudder,* 193: St Nikodimos's commentary on the 9th Canon of the Fourth Ecumenical Council.

87   Ibid., 177–8.

88   bid., 177.

89   Rallis, Potlis, *Constitution of the Divine and Holy Canons. Vol.2,* 133.

90   «Ἀνοικτή Ἐπιστολή γιά τό Οὐκρανικό Ζήτημα», *Παρακαταθήκη* [An Open Letter Regarding the Ukrainian Issue", *Parakatathiki Magazine,* #127] (July–August, 2019), 6.

91   ΧΡ. Α. ΠΑΠΑΔΟΠΟΥΛΟΥ, *Ἡ Ἐκκλησία τῆς Ἑλλάδος. Ἀπ' ἀρχῆς μέχρι τοῦ 1934,* [Archbishop of Athens and all Greece, Hristodoulos Papadopoulos, *The Church of Greece: From the Beginning to 1934*] (Athens, 2000), 220–4.

92   *Ἡ Συνθήκη τῆς Λωζάνης. Τό πλῆρες κείμενο - Προσθῆκες - Ἑρμηνευτικές διατάξεις, ἐκ τοῦ Ἐθνικοῦ Τυπογραφείου,* [The Treaty of Lausanne, the Full Text with Commentary] (Athens, 1923).

93   Γ. ΑΝΔΡΟΥΤΣΟΠΟΥΛΟΥ, «Τουρκική Ἐπέμβαση στό Πατριαρχεῖο» [G. Androutsopoulos, "Turkish Interference in the Patriarchate"] October 15, 2018, *http//www.kathimerini.2r/989769/gallery/toyrkikh-epemvash-sto-patriar-xeio*

94   ΑΝ. ΒΑΒΟΥΣΚΟΥ, «Περί συμμετοχῆς τῶν Μητροπολιτῶν τῶν Νέων Χωρῶν στή σύνθεση τῆς Ἱερᾶς Συνόδου τοῦ Οἰκουμενικοῦ Πατριαρχείου» [An. Babouskos, "On the Participation of the Metropolitans of the New Countries in the Synod of the Ecumenical Patriarchate"] August 7, 2018, *http://ortho doxia.info/news/περί-συμμετοχῆς-των- Μητροπολιτών-των*

95   Rallis, Potlis, *Constitution of the Divine and Holy Canons. Vol.2,* 14.

96   Ibid., 15.

97   Ibid., 124.

98   Nikodimos, *Rudder*, 407.

99   Ibid., 408.

100 ΒΑΡΘΟΛΟΜΑΙΟΥ, «Ἐπιστολή πρός τόν Ἀρχιεπίσκοπον Τιράνων καί πάσης Ἀλβανίας Ἀναστάσιον» [Bartholomew, Archbishop of Constantinople and Ecumenical Patriarch, "Letter to Archbishop Anastasios of Tirana and all Albania] February 20, 2019, *https://www.patriarchate.org/el/-/letter-to-archbishop-of-albania-2019-01-14*

101 Π. Ι. ΜΠΟΥΜΗ, «Παρατηρήσεις στόν Τόμο Αὐτοκεφαλίας τῆς Οὐκρανικῆς Ἐκκλησίας», [P.I Boumis: *Notes on the Ukrainian Church's Tome of Autocephaly*] January 24, 2019, https://www.romfea. gr/ katigories/10-apopseis/26620-paratiriseis-ston-tomo   -autokefalias-tis-oukranikis-ekklisias

102 Θ. ΓΙΑΓΚΟΥ, «Ἀπό τή Σύνοδο τῆς Κρήτης στήν Αὐτοκεφαλία τῆς ἐν Οὐκρανίᾳ Ἐκκλησίας», [Giagkos, "From the Synod of Crete to the Autocephaly of the Ukrainian Church"] November 29, 2019, orthodoxia. info/news/ἀπό-τη-σύνοδο-της-Κρήτης-στην-αυτοκεφα/

103 Ibid.

104 *"Four* Metropolitans Request ... " 2019.

105 DOSITHEOS (Patriarch of Jerusalem), *Ἱστορία περί τῶν ἐν Ἱεροσολύμοις Πατριαρχευσάντων, διηρημένη ἐν δώδεκα βιβλίοις, ἄλλως καλουμένη Δωδεκάβιβλος,* [*History of the Patriarchs of Jerusalem, Divided into 12 Books, Otherwise Known as the Dodekabiblos (twelvebooks)*] Volume I (Books I and II), (Thessaloniki, 1982), 283.

106 Nikodim Milaš, *Τό Ἐκκλησιαστικόν Δίκαιον τῆς Ὀρθοδόξου Ἀνατολικῆς Ἐκκλησίας* [*The Ecclesiastical Law of the Eastern Orthodox Church*] (Athens, 1906), 289–91.

107 Ibid., 194–5.

108 Nikodemos, *Rudder*, 193. Commentary on Canon 9 of the Fourth Ecumenical Council.

109 *Ἐγκύκλιος. Πατριαρχική καί Συνοδική Ἐπιστολή, πρός τούς Ἱερωτάτους καί Θεοφιλεστάτους, ἐν Χριστῷ Ἀδελφούς, Μητροπολίτας καί Ἐπισκόπους, καί τόν περί αὐτούς Ἱερόν καί Εὐαγῆ Κλῆρον, καί ἄπαν τό εὐσεβές καί Ὀρθόδοξον πλήρωμα τοῦ Ἁγιωτάτου Ἀποστολικοῦ καί Πατριαρχικοῦ Θρόνου Κωνσταντινουπόλεως* [*Patriarchal Encyclical and Synodal Letter to the Most Holy Brothers in Christ, Beloved by God, Metropolitans and Bishops, and with*

Them the Holy Clerics, and the Whole Pious and Orthodox Flock of the Most
Holy Apostolic and Patriarchal Throne of Constantinople] (Constantinople,
1895), 10–11.

110   Fidas, *The Ecumenical Patriarchate*, 33.

111   Ibid.

112   Fidas, *The Synodical Act of the Ecumenical Patriarchate*. 2018.

113   Κ. ΜΟΥΡΑΤΙΔΟΥ, *Κανονικόν Δίκαιον, Πανεπιστημιακαί Παραδόσεις* (K.
Mouratidis, *Canon Law: University Traditions*] (Athens, 1972), 171.

114   Ibid., 169–70.

115   Π. Ι. ΜΠΟΥΜΗ, «Τό πολίτευμα τῆς Ὀρθόδοξης Ἐκκλησίας», [P. Boumis,
"The System of Governance of the Orthodox Church"] December 4, 2019,
*www.romfea.gr/epikairotita-xronika/33524-to-poli   teuma-tis-orthodojis-
ekklisias*

116   Ibid.

117   ΙΩ. ΧΡΥΣΟΣΤΟΜΟΥ, *Εἰς τόν ρμθ΄ ψαλμόν*, [Chrysostom, *On
Psalm 149*] PG 55, 493. See also. ΙΕΡΟΘΕΟΥ, «Ὁ ὅρος "Αὐτοκέφαλη
Ἐκκλησία"», [Metropolitan Ierotheos of Nafpaktos and St. Blaise, "The
Term 'Autocephalous Church'"] June 27, 2019. *Othodoxianewsagency.
gr/mitropolitiko_ergo/ι-μ-ναυπάκτου-και-αγίου-βλασίου/sevasmiotatou-
naypaktou-ierotheou-o-oros-aytokefali-ekklisia/*

118   Milaš, *The Ecclesiastical Law*, 444.

119   Nikodimos, *Rudder*, 41

120   Ibid., 41.

121   Ibid., 128.

122   Ibid., 201.

123   Ibid., 225–6.

124   bid., 327.

125   Ibid., 36.

126   Ibid., 37.

127   ΑΝ. ΒΑΒΟΥΣΚΟΥ, «Ἡ Πανορθόδοξη ἀντιμετώπιση τοῦ "Οὐκρανικοῦ" ὡς
ἰδέα καί ὡς πραγματικότητα» [Anastasios Babouskos, "The Panorthodox
Response to the Ukrainian Issue, as an Idea, and as Reality"] December
3, 2019, *https://www.romfea.gr/katigories/10-apopseis/33510-i -panorthodoji-
antimetopisi-tou-oukranikou-os-idea-kai-os-pragmatikotita*

128   Nikodimos, *Rudder*, 37.

129   *Constitutional Charter of the Most Holy Church of Cyprus*, 16–17.

130   «Μήνυμα τῆς Ἁγίας καί Μεγάλης Συνόδου τῆς Ὀρθοδόξου Ἐκκλησίας. Πρός τόν Ὀρθόδοξο λαό καί κάθε ἄνθρωπο καλῆς θελήσεως», *Ἀπόστολος Βαρνάβας*, περίοδος Δ΄, τόμος 77ος [Message from the Great and Holy Synod of the Orthodox Church to the Orthodox People and Every Well-Intentioned Individual." *Apostle Barnabas Magazine*, Period 4, volume 77] (May–June 2016), 317. [English version: https://www.holycouncil.org/-/message].

131   Θ. Ν. ΖΗΣΗ (Πρωτ.), «Τό Οὐκρανικό Αὐτοκέφαλο. Ἀπόκρυψη καί παρερμηνεία ἐγγράφων», 2 Νοεμβρίου 2018, *https://www.romfea.gr/epikairotita-xronika/24774-to-oukraniko-autokefalo-apokrupsi-kai-parermineia-eggrafon*

132   «Διεθνές Συνέδριο: Ἡ θεολογική παρακαταθήκη τοῦ Πρωθιερέως Γεωργίου Φλωρόφσκυ», ["International Congress: The Theological Legacy of Georges Florovsky"] September 2, 2019, *https://www.romfea.gr/oikoumeniko-patriarxeio/31285-diethnes-sunedrio-i-theologiki-parakatathiki-tou-prothiereos-georgiou-florofsku*

133   ΝΙΚΟΛΑΟΥ (Μητροπολίτου Μεσογαίας καί Λαυρεωτικῆς), «Διχασμένοι Αὐτοκέφαλοι ἤ Ἑνωμένοι Ἀδελφοί;» [Metropolitan Nicholas of Mesogeia, "Divided Autocephaly, or United Brotherhood?"] October 24, 2018. *https://www.romfea.gr/epikairotita-xronika/24589-mesogaias-nikolaos-dixasmenoi-autokefaloi-i-enomenoi-adelfoi*

134   Α. ΤΡΙΑΝΤΑΦΥΛΛΟΥ, «Βαρθολομαῖος: Ἡ διαίρεσις δίδει ὤθησιν διά τήν ἀποκατάστασιν τῆς ἑνότητος» ["Bartholomew: The Division Gives Impetus for the Restoration of Unity"], 30 Νοεμβρίου 2019, *orthodoxia.info/news/πατριάρχης-σε-αντιπροσωπεία-του-βατι/*

135   Giagkos, "From the Synod of Crete … " 2019.

136   ΕΛΠΙΔΟΦΟΡΟΥ, «Ὁ Ἐνθρονιστήριος Λόγος», [Elpidoforos, "Enthronement Address"] Jun. 22, 2019. *https://www.orthodoxianewsagency.gr/patriarxeia/oikomeniko_patriarxio/αρχιεπισκο πή-αμερικής/o-enthronistirios-logos-tou-arxiep-amerikis/*[English: https://www.goarch.org/-/enthronement-address-archbishop-elpidophoros]

137   Α. ΠΑΥΛΙΔΗ, *Ἡ Κωνσταντίνου Πόλις, Ἱστορία, Περιγραφή, Θρύλοι (καί σύντομη Ἱστορία τῆς Βυζαντινῆς Αὐτοκρατορίας)*, τόμος Β΄ [A. Pavlidis, *The City of Constantine: History, Description, Legends, and a Short History of the Byzantine Empire*] (Lefkosia, Cyprus. 2005), 13.

138   ΣΠ. ΠΑΠΑΓΕΩΡΓΙΟΥ, «Εὐθεία ἀμφισβήτηση τοῦ Οἰκουμενικοῦ Πατριάρχη ἀπό τόν Μπάτσκας Εἰρηναῖο» [Sp. Papageorgiou, "Irinej of Bačka Against the Claims of the Ecumenical Patriarch"] Jan. 1, 2020, *https://orthodoxia.info/news/ευθεία-αμφισβήτηση-του-οικουμενικού/*

139   Θ. Ν. ΖΗΣΗ, «Τό Οὐκρανικό Αὐτοκέφαλο. Ἀπόκρυψη καί παρερμηνεία ἐγγράφων», [Zisis, "Ukrainian Autocephaly, "Withholding and Misinterpreting the Documents"] Nov. 2, 2018, *https://www.romfea. gr/epikairotita-xronika/24774-to-oukrani   ko-autokefalo-apokrupsi   -kai- parermineia-eggrafon*

140   See ΑΔ. Δ. ΑΠΟΣΤΟΛΟΠΟΥΛΟΥ (Ἀρχιμ.), *Ὀρθοδοξίας Μηνύματα,* [Archmandrite A. Apostolopoulos, *Orthodox Messages*] (Athens 1978), 146.

141   Ibid.

142   «Δήλωση τῆς Ἱερᾶς Συνόδου τῆς Ὀρθοδόξου Ἐκκλησίας τῆς Ρωσίας, σχετικά μέ τήν ἀπόφαση τῶν Τουρκικῶν Ἀρχῶν νά ἀναθεωρήσουν τό καθεστώς τοῦ Ναοῦ τῆς Ἁγίας Σοφίας», [Statement from the Holy Synod of the Orthodox Church of Russia regarding the Turkish Authorities' Decision to Revisit the status of the Church of Hagia Sophia"] July 17, 2020, *https://mospat.ru/gr/2020/07/17/news185467/*[English version: https:// mospat.ru/en/news/45480/]

143   «Δήλωση τοῦ Πατριάρχη Μόσχας καί Πασῶν τῶν Ρωσιῶν Κυρίλλου» [Statement from Kirill, Patriarch of Moscow and all Russia"] July 6, 2020, *http://www.patri*archia.ru/gr/db/text/5659216.html   [English version: http://www.patriarchia.ru/en/db/text/5659218.html]

Bibliography

«Ἀνοικτή Ἐπιστολή γιά τό Οὐκρανικό Ζήτημα», Πα- ρακαταθήκη, τεῦχος 127 (Ἰούλιος-Αὔγουστος 2019), σσ. 3-10.

«Αὐτοκεφαλία τῆς Ἐκκλησίας τῆς Οὐκρανίας. Εἰσή- γησις τοῦ Μακαριωτάτου Ἀρχιεπισκόπου Ἀθηνῶν καί πάσης Ἑλλάδος Ἱερωνύμου (12 Ὀκτωβρίου 2019)», Ἐκκλησία, τόμος 96ος (Ὀκτώβριος 2019), σσ. 853-856.

«Δήλωση τῆς Ἱερᾶς Συνόδου τῆς Ὀρθοδόξου Ἐκ- κλησίας τῆς Ρωσίας γιά τήν παράνομη εἰσπήδηση τοῦ Πατριαρχείου Κωνσταντινουπόλεως στό κανονικό ἔδα- φος τῆς Ὀρθοδόξου Ἐκκλησίας τῆς Ρωσίας», 14 Σε- πτεμβρίου 2018, http://www.patriarchia.ru/gr/db/text/ 5268288.html

«Δήλωση τῆς Ἱερᾶς Συνόδου τῆς Ὀρθοδόξου Ἐκ- κλησίας τῆς Ρωσίας», 17 Ὀκτωβρίου 2019, https://mo spat.ru/gr/2019/10/17/news178948/

«Δήλωση τοῦ Πατριάρχη Μόσχας καί Πασῶν τῶν Ρωσιῶν Κυρίλλου», 6 Ἰουλίου 2020, http://www.patri archia.ru/gr/db/text/5659216.html

«Δήλωση τῆς Ἱερᾶς Συνόδου τῆς Ὀρθοδόξου Ἐκ- κλησίας τῆς Ρωσίας, σχετικά μέ τήν ἀπόφαση τῶν Τουρ κικῶν Ἀρχῶν νά ἀναθεωρήσουν τό καθεστώς τοῦ Ναοῦ τῆς Ἁγίας Σοφίας», 17 Ἰουλίου 2020, https://mospat.ru/ gr/2020/07/17/news185467

«Διεθνές Συνέδριο: Ἡ θεολογική παρακαταθήκη τοῦ Πρωθιερέως Γεωργίου Φλωρόφσκυ», 2 Σεπτεμβρί- ου 2019, https://www.romfea.gr/ oikoumeniko-patriarx eio/31285-diethnes-sunedrio-i-theologiki-parakatathi ki-tou-prothiereos-georgiou-florofsku

Ἐγκύκλιος. Πατριαρχική καί Συνοδική Ἐπιστολή, πρός τούς Ἱερωτάτους καί Θεοφιλεστάτους, ἐν Χριστῷ Ἀδελ- φούς, Μητροπολίτας καί Ἐπισκόπους, καί τόν περί αὐτούς Ἱερόν καί Εὐαγῆ Κλῆρον, καί ἅπαν τό εὐσεβές καί Ὀρθό- δοξον πλήρωμα τοῦ Ἁγιωτάτου Ἀποστολικοῦ καί Πατριαρ- χικοῦ Θρόνου Κωνσταντινουπόλεως, ἐκ τοῦ Πατριαρχι- κοῦ Τυπογραφείου, ἐν Κωνσταντινουπόλει 1895.

«Ἐπιστολή Μητροπολίτη Βιδυνίου Δανιήλ στούς Ἱεράρχες τῶν Ἐκκλησιῶν γιά τό Οὐκρανικό», 19 Ἰου- νίου 2019, https://spzh.news/gr/zashhita-very/62935-obrashhenije-mitropolita-vidinskogo-ijerarkham-cerk vej-po-ukrainskoj-probleme

Ἡ Συνθήκη τῆς Λωζάνης. Τό πλῆρες κείμενο - Προ- σθῆκες - Ἑρμηνευτικές διατάξεις, ἐκ τοῦ Ἐθνικοῦ Τυ- πογραφείου, ἐν Ἀθήναις 1923, ἀνατύπωση, ἐφημ. «Τά Νέα», Ἀθήνα 2018. Καταστατικός Χάρτης τῆς Ἁγιωτάτης Ἐκκλησίας τῆς Κύπρου, Λευκωσία 2010.

«Μήνυμα τῆς Ἁγίας καί Μεγάλης Συνόδου τῆς Ὀρ- θοδόξου Ἐκκλησίας. Πρός τόν Ὀρθόδοξο λαό καί κάθε ἄνθρωπο καλῆς θελήσεως», Ἀπόστολος Βαρνάβας, πε- ρίοδος Δ΄, τόμος 77ος (Μάιος-Ἰούνιος 2016), σσ. 316- 321. Ὀρθοδοξία 36 (1961), σσ. 303-304.

«Σύγκληση Πανορθόδοξης Συνόδου γιά τό Οὐκρα- νικό ζητοῦν 4 Μητροπολίτες (Κονίτσης Ἀνδρέας, Πει- ραιῶς Σεραφείμ, Κηθύρων Σεραφείμ καί Αἰτωλίας Κο- σμᾶς)», 29 Νοεμβρίου 2019, www.ethnos.gr/ekklisia /ekklisia-tis-ellados/74798_sygklisi-panorthodoxis-synodoy-gia-oykraniko-zitoyn-4

«Χρησιμοποιούμεναι ξενόγλωσσοι φράσεις (ἐκ τῆς Λατινικῆς καί ἄλλων γλωσσῶν)», Νεώτερον Ἐγκυκλο- παιδικόν Λεξικόν Ἡλίου, τόμος 18ος, Ἀθῆναι χ.χ., σσ. 1047-1053.

ΑΓΑΠΙΟΥ ΙΕΡΟΜΟΝΑΧΟΥ ΚΑΙ ΝΙΚΟΔΗΜΟΥ ΜΟΝΑΧΟΥ, Πηδάλιον, ἐν Ζακύνθῳ 1864, ἀνατύπω- σις, ἐκδ. «Ἀστήρ», Ἀθῆναι 1957.

ΑΛΙΒΙΖΑΤΟΥ Α. Σ., Οἱ Ἱεροί Κανόνες καί οἱ Ἐκκλη σιαστικοί Νόμοι, Βιβλιοθήκη Ἀποστολικῆς Διακονίας, ἐν Ἀθήναις 2 1949.

ΑΝΔΡΟΥΤΣΟΠΟΥΛΟΥ Γ., «Τουρκική Ἐπέμβαση στό Πατριαρχεῖο», 15 Ὀκτωβρίου 2018, http//www.kathi merini.2r/989769/gallery/toyrkikh-epemvash-sto-patri ar-xeio

ΑΠΟΣΤΟΛΟΠΟΥΛΟΥ ΑΔ. Δ. (Ἀρχιμ.), Ὀρθοδοξίας Μηνύματα, χ.ἐ., Ἀθῆναι 1978.

ΒΑΒΟΥΣΚΟΥ ΑΝ., «Περί συμμετοχῆς τῶν Μη- τροπολιτῶν τῶν Νέων Χωρῶν στή σύνθεση τῆς Ἱερᾶς Συνόδου τοῦ Οἰκουμενικοῦ Πατριαρχείου», 7 Αὐγού- στου 2018, http://orthodoxia.info/news/περί-συμμετο χῆς-των-Μητροπολιτών-των

ΤΟΥ ΙΔΙΟΥ, «Ἡ Πανορθόδοξη ἀντιμετώπιση τοῦ "Οὐκρανικοῦ" ὡς ἰδέα καί ὡς πραγματικότητα», 3 Δε- κεμβρίου 2019, https://www.romfea.gr/katigories/10-apopseis/33510-i-panorthodoji-antimetopisi-tou-ou kranikou-os-idea-kai-os-pragmatikotita

ΒΑΡΘΟΛΟΜΑΙΟΥ (Ἀρχιεπισκόπου Κωνσταντι- νουπόλεως καί Οἰκουμενικοῦ Πατριάρχου), «Πρός τόν Οὐκρανικόν λαόν (26 Ἰουλίου 2008)», Ὀρθοδοξία, πε- ρίοδος Β΄, ἔτος ΙΕ΄, τεῦχος Γ΄ (Ἰούλιος-Σεπτέμβριος 2008), σσ. 527-535.

ΤΟΥ ΙΔΙΟΥ, «Ἐπιστολή πρός τόν Ἀρχιεπίσκοπον Τιράνων καί πάσης Ἀλβανίας Ἀναστάσιον», 20 Φε- βρουαρίου 2019, https://www.patriarchate.org/el/-/letter-to-archbishop-of-albania-2019-01-14

ΓΙΑΓΚΟΥ Θ., «Ἀπό τή Σύνοδο τῆς Κρήτης στήν Αὐτοκεφαλία τῆς ἐν Οὐκρανίᾳ Ἐκκλησίας», 29 Νοεμ- βρίου 2019, orthodoxia.info/news/ από-τη-σύνοδο-της-Κρήτης-στην-αυτοκεφα/

ΓΚΟΤΣΟΠΟΥΛΟΥ ΑΝ. Κ. (Πρωτ.), «Μικρή συμ-βολή στόν διάλογο γιά τό Οὐκρανικό "Αὐτοκέφαλο"», 8 Ἰανουαρίου 2019, https://www.impantokratoros.gr/961 E0E58.el.aspx

ΤΟΥ ΙΔΙΟΥ, «Μικρή Συμβολή στόν διάλογο γιά τό Οὐκρανικό "Αὐτοκέφαλο" Β΄», 15 Μαρτίου 2019, https://mospat.ru/gr/ 2019/03/15/news171593/

ΤΟΥ ΙΔΙΟΥ, «Ἀπλές ἐρωτήσεις κατανόησις κειμέ- νου Β´», 22 Αὐγούστου 2019, https://www.romfea.gr/   epikairotita-xronika/31070-aples-erotiseis-katanoisis-keimenou-b

ΔΕΛΙΚΑΝΗ Κ. (Ἀρχιμ.), Τά ἐν τοῖς κώδιξι τοῦ Πα- τριαρχικοῦ Ἀρχειοφυλακίου σωζόμενα ἐπίσημα ἐκκλη- σιαστικά ἔγγραφα, τά ἀφορῶντα εἰς τάς σχέσεις τοῦ Οἰ- κουμενικοῦ Πατριαρχείου πρός τάς Ἐκκλησίας Ρωσσίας, Βλαχίας καί Μολδαβίας, Σερβίας, Ἀχριδῶν καί Πεκίου 1564-1863, τόμος Γ´, ἐκ τοῦ Πατριαρχικοῦ Τυπογρα- φείου, ἐν Κωνσταντινουπόλει 1905.

ΔΟΣΙΘΕΟΥ (Πατριάρχου Ἱεροσολύμων), Ἱστορία περί τῶν ἐν Ἱεροσολύμοις Πατριαρχευσάντων, διηρημένη ἐν δώδεκα βιβλίοις, ἄλλως καλουμένη Δωδεκάβιβλος, τόμος Α´ (βιβλία Α´ καί Β´), ἐκδ. «Ρηγοπούλου», Θεσ- σαλονίκη 1982.

ΕΛΠΙΔΟΦΟΡΟΥ (Ἀρχιεπισκόπου Ἀμερικῆς), «Ὁ Ἐνθρονιστήριος Λόγος», 22 Ἰουνίου 2019, https://www. orthodoxia newsagency.gr/patriarxeia/oikomeniko_ patriarxio /αρχιεπισκοπή-αμερικής/o-enthronistirios-logos-tou-arxiep-amerikis/

ΖΗΣΗ Θ. Ν. (Πρωτ.), Κωνσταντινούπολη καί Μό- σχα, ἐκδ. «Βρυέννιος», Θεσσαλονίκη 1989.

ΤΟΥ ΙΔΙΟΥ, «Τό Οὐκρανικό Αὐτοκέφαλο. Ἀπόκρυ- ψη καί παρερμηνεία ἐγγράφων», 2 Νοεμβρίου 2018, https://www.romfea.gr/epikairotita-xronika/24774-to-oukraniko-autokefalo-apokrupsi-kai-parermineia-eggrafon

ΤΟΥ ΙΔΙΟΥ, Τό Οὐκρανικό Αὐτοκέφαλο, ἐκδ. «Τό Παλίμψηστον», Θεσσαλονίκη 2019.

ΘΕΟΤΟΚΑ Γ., Ἡ Ὀρθοδοξία στόν καιρό μας - Δο-κίμια, «Οἱ Ἐκδόσεις τῶν Φίλων», Ἀθήνα 1975.

ΙΕΡΟΘΕΟΥ (Μητροπολίτου Ναυπάκτου καί Ἁγίου Βλασίου), «Ὁ ὅρος "Αὐτοκέφαλη Ἐκκλησία"», 27 Ἰου-νίου 2019, othodoxianewsagency,gr/ mitropolitiko_ ergo/ι-μ-ναυπάκτου-και-αγίου-βλασίου/sevasmiotatou -naypaktou-ierotheou-o-oros-aytokefali-ekklisia/

ΚΩΝΣΤΑΝΤΕΛΟΥ Δ. ΙΩ. (Πρωτ.), Ἐθνική ταυτό-τητα καί Θρησκευτική ἰδιαιτερότητα τοῦ Ἑλληνισμοῦ, ἐκδ. «Δαμασκός», Ἀθῆναι 1993.

ΜΕΛΕΤΗ Γ. Β., Διάλογος μέ τόν οὐρανό, Ἀδελφό-της Θεολόγων ἡ «Ζωή», Ἀθῆναι 1974.

ΜΙΛΑ ΝΙΚΟΔΗΜΟΥ (Ἐπισκόπου Ζάρας τῆς Δαλ- ματικῆς), Τό Ἐκκλησιαστικόν Δίκαιον τῆς Ὀρθοδόξου Ἀνατολικῆς Ἐκκλησίας, Τύποις «Π.Δ. Σακελλαρίου», ἐν Ἀθήναις 1906.

ΜΟΥΡΑΤΙΔΟΥ Κ. (Καθηγητοῦ Πανεπιστημίου Ἀθηνῶν), Κανονικόν Δίκαιον, Πανεπιστημιακαί Παρα-δόσεις, Ἀθῆναι 1972.

ΜΠΟΥΜΗ Π. Ι. (Καθηγητῆ Πανεπιστημίου Ἀθηνῶν), Ἡ ἀκρίβεια καί ἡ ἀλήθεια τῶν Ἱερῶν Κανόνων (Ἐπιστασία - ἑρμηνευτικόν γύμνασμα ἐπί τῶν 91ου καί 92ου Κανόνων τοῦ Μ. Βασιλείου), ἐκδ. «Ἐπέκταση», Κα-τερίνη 1996.

ΤΟΥ ΙΔΙΟΥ, «Παρατηρήσεις στόν Τόμο Αὐτοκεφα-λίας τῆς Οὐκρανικῆς Ἐκκλησίας», 24 Ἰανουαρίου 2019, https://www.romfea.gr /katigories/10-apopseis/26620 paratiriseis-ston-tomo-autokefalias-tis-oukranikis-ekklisias

ΤΟΥ ΙΔΙΟΥ, «Τό πολίτευμα τῆς Ὀρθόδοξης Ἐκκλη-σίας», 4 Δεκεμβρίου 2019, www.romfea.gr/epikairoti ta-xronika/33524-to-politeuma-tis-orthodojis-ekklisias

ΝΙΚΟΛΑΟΥ (Μητροπολίτου Μεσογαίας καί Λαυ-ρεωτικῆς), «Διχασμένοι Αὐτοκέφαλοι ἤ Ἑνωμένοι Ἀδελ-φοί;», 24 Ὀκτωβρίου 2018, https://www. romfea.gr/epi kairotita-xronika/24589-mesogaias-nikolaos-dixasme noi-autokefaloi-i-enomenoi-adelfoi

ΠΑΝΑΓΙΩΤΑΚΟΥ Π. Ι., Σύστημα τοῦ Ἐκκλησια-στικοῦ Δικαίου, τόμος Γ΄, Τό Ποινικό Δίκαιο τῆς Ἐκκλη-σίας, ἐκδ. Μυρτίδης, Ἀθῆναι 1962.

ΠΑΠΑΓΕΩΡΓΙΟΥ ΣΠ., «Εὐθεία ἀμφισβήτηση τοῦ Οἰκουμενικοῦ Πατριάρχη ἀπό τόν Μπάτσκας Εἰρηναῖο», 1η Ἰανουαρίου 2020, https://orthodoxia. info/news/ ευθεία-αμφισβήτηση-του-οικουμενικού/

ΠΑΠΑΔΟΠΟΥΛΟΥ ΧΡ. Α. (Ἀρχιεπισκόπου Ἀθη- νῶν καί πάσης Ἑλλάδος), Ἡ Ἐκκλησία τῆς Ἑλλάδος. Ἀπ᾽ ἀρχῆς μέχρι τοῦ 1934, Ἀποστολική Διακονία, Ἀθῆναι 32000 (σέ μεταγλώττιση).

ΠΑΠΟΥΤΣΟΠΟΥΛΟΥ ΧΡ. Ν. (Ἀρχιμ.), Λόγοι τῆς Χάριτος, Ἀδελφότης Θεολόγων «ὁ Σωτήρ», Ἀθῆναι 21969.

ΠΑΣΧΟΥ Π. Β., Ὁ διάλογος μέ τή Δύση γιά τό Θεό καί τόν ἄνθρωπο - Ἡ ποιητική θεολογία τοῦ Pavel Nico-laievitch Evdokimov, ἐκδ. «Ἁρμός», Ἀθήνα 1995.

ΠΑΥΛΙΔΗ Α., Ἡ Κωνσταντίνου Πόλις, Ἱστορία, Πε-ριγραφή, Θρύλοι (καί σύντομη Ἱστορία τῆς Βυζαντινῆς Αὐτοκρατορίας), τόμος Β΄, ἐκδ. «Φιλόκυπρος», Λευκω-σία - Κύπρος 2005.

ΠΟΛΥΓΕΝΗ ΑΙΜ., «Διοκλείας Κάλλιστος (Ware): Δέν συμφωνῶ μέ τό Φανάρι ἀλλά οὔτε μέ τήν Μόσχα», 14 Δεκεμβρίου 2018, https://www.romfea.gr/ sinentey xeis/25730-diokleias-kallistos-ware-den-sumfono-me -to-fanari- alla-oute-me-tin-mosxa-

ΡΑΛΛΗ Γ. Α. - ΠΟΤΛΗ Μ., Σύνταγμα Θείων καί Ἱερῶν Κανόνων τῶν τε Ἁγίων καί Πανευφήμων Ἀποστό-λων, καί τῶν Ἱερῶν Οἰκουμενικῶν καί Τοπικῶν Συνό-δων, καί τῶν κατά μέρος Ἁγίων Πατέρων, τόμος Β΄, ἐκτῆς Τυπογραφίας «Γ. Χαρτοφύλακος», Ἀθήνησιν 1852.

ΣΕΡΑΦΕΙΜ (Μητροπολίτου Πειραιῶς), «Ποτέ δέν ἀποδέχθηκα πρόταση, γιά ἀναγνώριση τῆς ἀνυπόστα- της "Ἐκκλησίας", πού δημιουργήθηκε στήν Οὐκρανία», 13 Ὀκτωβρίου 2019, https://www.romfea.gr/epikairo tita-xronika/32274-peiraios-pote-den-apodexthika-pro tasi-gia-anagnorisi-tis-anupostatis-ekklisias-pou-dimi ourgithike-stin-oukrania

ΣΟΥΜΙΛΟ Σ. (Διευθυντοῦ τοῦ ἐν Κιέβῳ Διεθνοῦς Ἰνστιτούτου τῆς Ἁγιορειτικῆς Κληρονομίας), «Ἕνα πα-λαιό πρόβλημα τῆς νέας Ἐκκλησίας. Τό Κίνημα τοῦ Λιπκόφσκι ὡς πνευματικό, κανονικό καί ἐκκλησιολογικό πρόβλημα τῶν ἐν Οὐκρανίᾳ Ἐκκλησιῶν», 2 Ἰουνίου 2020, https://www.romfea.gr/katigories/10-apopseis/ 29502-ena-palaio-problima-tis-neas-ekklisias

ΣΤΑΥΡΙΔΟΥ Β., Συνοπτική Ἱστορία τοῦ Οἰκουμενι-κοῦ Πατριαρχείου, Πατριαρχικό Ἵδρυμα Πατερικῶν Μελετῶν, Θεσσαλονίκη 1991.

ΣΤΕΦΑΝΙΔΟΥ Β. Κ. (Ἀρχιμ.), Ἐκκλησιαστική Ἱστο-ρία, ἀπ᾽ ἀρχῆς μέχρι σήμερον, ἐκδ. «Ἀστήρ», Ἀθῆναι 21959.

ΤΖΩΡΤΖΑΤΟΥ Β. Δ. (Μητροπολίτου Κίτρους), Οἱ βασικοί θεσμοί διοικήσεως τῶν Ὀρθοδόξων Πατριαρ-χείων, μετά ἱστορικῶν ἀνασκοπήσεων, Ἑταιρεία Μακεδονικῶν Σπουδῶν - Ἵδρυμα Μελετῶν Χερσονήσου τοῦ Αἵμου, ἐν Ἀθήναις 1972.

ΤΡΙΑΝΤΑΦΥΛΛΟΥ Α., «Βαρθολομαῖος: Ἡ διαίρε-σις δίδει ὤθησιν διά τήν ἀποκατάστασιν τῆς ἑνότητος», 30 Νοεμβρίου 2019, orthodoxia.info/news/πατριάρχης -σε-αντιπροσωπεία-του-βατι/

ΦΕΙΔΑ ΒΛ. ΙΩ., «Τό "Αὐτοκέφαλον" καί τό "Αὐτό-νομον" ἐν τῇ Ὀρθοδόξῳ Ἐκκλησίᾳ», Νέα Σιών, ἔτος οα΄, τεῦχος Α΄ (Ἰανουάριος - Ἰούνιος 1979), σσ. 9-32.

ΤΟΥ ΙΔΙΟΥ, «Τό Οἰκουμενικό Πατριαρχεῖο. Ἡ δια-χρονική ἐκκλησιαστική διακονία του», Τό Οἰκουμενικό Πατριαρχεῖο - Ἡ Μεγάλη τοῦ Χριστοῦ Ἐκκλησία, Ὀρθόδοξο Κέντρο Οἰκουμενικοῦ Πατριαρχείου Γενεύης, Ἑλβετία - Ἐ. Τζαφέρη Α.Ε., Ἀθήνα 1989, σσ. 11-43.

ΤΟΥ ΙΔΙΟΥ, Ἐκκλησιαστική Ἱστορία τῆς Ρωσίας (988-1988), Ἀποστολική Διακονία τῆς Ἐκκλησίας τῆς Ἑλλάδος, Ἀθῆναι 31988.

ΤΟΥ ΙΔΙΟΥ, «Ἡ Συνοδική Πράξη τοῦ Οἰκουμενικοῦ Πατριαρχείου (1686) καί ἡ Αὐτοκεφαλία τῆς Ἐκκλησίας Οὐκρανίας», 28 Νοεμβρίου 2018, https:// orthodoxia. info/news/h-συνοδική-πράξη-του-οικουμενικού -πατρ/

ΧΡΥΣΟΣΤΟΜΟΥ ΙΩ., Εἰς τόν ρμθ΄ ψαλμόν, PG 55, 493-495.

ΤΟΥ ΙΔΙΟΥ, Ὁμιλία ΙΑ΄ εἰς τήν πρός Ἐφεσίους Ἐπι-στολήν, PG 62, 79-88.

Index

A

Afanasiev, Nikolai 20

Africa 33, 35, 36

African bishops 33

Alivizatos, Amilkas 19, 98

Anastasios, Archbishop of Albania 5, 52, 70, 96, 101–2

anathematization 7, 8

Anatolios, archbishop of Constantinople 38

Anthimos, Ecumenical Patriarch 59

anti-canonical xi, 22, 88, 91

Antioch 2, 3, 16, 42–4, 49, 50, 60, 68, 74, 95

Apostolic Canons 42, 51, 74

apostolic succession 26, 46

appeals xxiv, 31–4, 36, 37, 39, 40–1, 45, 73, 89

Armenia 83

Asia xix, 36, 48

Athanasius the Great 85

Athenagoras, Ecumenical Patriarch 21, 98

Australia 26

autocephalous church xviii, xxiv, xx, 5, 14, 16, 28-9, 31, 36, 52–3, 58, 72–4

autocephaly xi, xiii, xvii, xx, xxi, xxii, xxiv, 3, 8, 12, 15, 21–30, 42, 44–5, 47, 53–4, 60–1, 72–4, 78, 80, 83–4, 88, 91, 96, 121, 124

autonomy xx, 21, 23

B

Balkan Wars 48

Barnabas, Apostle vii, xxi, 43, 45, 65, 103

Bartholomew, Ecumenical Patriarch xvii, xxi, xxii, xxiv, 2, 6, 7, 8, 9, 12, 13, 21, 22, 24, 27, 29, 30, 47, 60–1, 73, 75, 77, 80, 96, 101, 103

Basil the Great 57

Panagiotis Boumis 53, 64

Brotherhood of the Workers of the Word 27

Bulgarian Exarchate 61

Byzantine Empire xix, 103

C

Canon Law 19–20, 40, 50, 55

canonical v, ix, xi, xiii, xx–xxiv, 1, 3, 4–9, 11, 12, 14–6, 20, 22, 23–9, 31, 33, 35, 37, 40–1, 44, 46, 49, 50, 52, 54, 58, 60–1, 72, 73, 75, 76, 77, 83, 85, 86, 88, 91, 98, 121, 123, 124

    dependence 2, 8, 15, 44

    judgment 8, 31, 34, 35, 40, 66

113

A Short Biography
of Metropolitan Nikiphoros
# of Kykkos and Tylliria, Cyprus

His Eminence Metropolitan of Kykkos and Tylliria, Nikiforos abbot of the renowned Kykkos monastery was born in the village of Kritou Marottou in Cyprus in 1947. He became a novice at the Kykkos monastery at a young age, was ordained a deacon in 1969 and entered the Law School of the University of Thessaloniki. After graduation in 1974 he entered theological seminary graduating in 1978. He was ordained to the priesthood in 1979 and subsequently elevated to the rank of archimandrite.

In 1984 he was enthroned abbot of Kykkos monastery. In 2002, he was chosen as bishop of Kykkos by the Holy Synod of the Church of Cyprus, and, in 2007 was unanimously elected metropolitan of the bishopric of Kykkos and Tylliyria.

Metropolitan Nikiforos is a member of the Council of the University of Cyprus and involved with various works including the establishment of the Holy Monastery of Kykkos Research Centre; the operation of a modern ecclesiastical museum in the central monastery; the operation of the the Most Holy

Theotokos Eleousa of Kykkos Foundation (*Eleousa* refers to the icon of the Virgin of Tenderness) for the accommodation of adults with mental and/or physical disabilities; and the continued development of theological studies in Cyprus. The Department of Theology of the University of Nicosia is under his supervision.

For his ecclesiastical, social, and cultural work he has been honored by many bodies. In 2001, the Municipality of Athens bestowed on him its highest distinction, the Golden Key to the City. He has also been awarded Honorary Doctorates from the Department of Pastoral and Social Theology of the Aristotle University Of Thessaloniki and the Department of Social Theology of the National and Kapodistrian University of Athens.

Endorsements

This book is a thoughtful and objective treatise for understanding the ecclesiastical crisis that has been created by the Ecumenical Patriarchate's granting autocephaly to schismatic groups in Ukraine, an action which has divided the Orthodox Church, with the evident risk of consolidating a wider schism, and that until today has not brought about the expected results of restoring the unity of the Orthodox faithful there.

The distinguished and learned Cypriot Hierarch, lifted to the height of his hierarchical conscience and responsibility, with profound theological knowledge and canonical seriousness, analyzes in detail the historical origin of the schism in Ukraine. He unimpeachably cites significant evidence about ecclesiastical jurisdiction from the Church's longstanding canonical order and flawlessly asks crucial questions about the canonicity a) of the situation that the Ecumenical Patriarchate has brought about in Ukraine and b) the "novel theories" that it has promoted regarding its special privileges, alien to Orthodox ecclesiology.

In this book, it becomes manifestly clear that Metropolitan Nikiforos, in a spirit of the love of Christ, is deeply concerned for the necessary cooperation and concord among the

Orthodox. In order to address the various challenges of the contemporary era, he worthily suggests commencing a crucial and honest dialogue through the convening of a Pan-Orthodox Synaxis of the primates of the Churches by the Ecumenical Patriarch. Its purpose would be to prevent further tension in relations between the Orthodox and to restore Eucharistic communion among them.

+TIMOTHEOS, Metropolitan of Bostra,
Patriarchate of Jerusalem

The Serbian Orthodox Church has always taken the position in support of proper Church order and the Holy Canons. We do not take the position of Greeks or Russians, rather we stand for what is just and right. Regarding the situation in the Ukraine, we cannot condone the rejection of the universally recognized status of the canonical Ukrainian Orthodox Church under the omophorion of Metropolitan Onuphry of Kiev. This situation in which we Orthodox have found ourselves is completely unnatural and does not serve the good of the Orthodox Church, rather it is contrary to it. We pray to the Almighty God and the Most-Holy Theotokos that this division ends quickly and Church order will reign again. We are pleased that writings such as this work by Metropolitan Nikiforos are working towards this correction.

+ LONGIN, Bishop of New Gracanica and Midwestern America,
Patriarchate of Serbia

The Orthodox Church of Poland is not against granting autocephaly to the Orthodox Church in Ukraine on the basis of the dogmatic and canonical norms which would apply to the entire Orthodox Church in Ukraine, and not for a schismatic group - roskolniki. A group separated from the teaching of the Holy Church cannot represent a healthy church organism, as this state violates the eucharistic unity of the Orthodoxy as a whole.

In this case, the penitential process of the "hierarchy" in the schism would be an indispensable act that should have taken place. Regretfully, these canonical and dogmatic norms were omitted, which caused, I hope only a temporary, crisis in the coexistence and conciliarity of local Orthodox churches.

This book addresses the many arguments and ways towards unity and the common Orthodox Church in Ukraine focused on serving God and His faithful. This lively analysis presents the situation of the Orthodox Church in Ukraine in an accessible way to both theologians, the faithful, and all people interested in the topic of the unity of the Orthodox Church in Ukraine.

+ABEL, Archbishop of Lublin and Chelm,
Orthodox Church of Poland

This is a serious study of a crisis in the life of our Orthodox Church worldwide that deserves to be widely read as we seek to understand the underlying issues more clearly and find a conciliar solution that brings both unity and peace. The author, His Eminence Nicephoros, the Metropolitan of Kykkos and the Abbot of the most prominent Cypriot monastery of the same name, is a hierarch widely known for his zealous care about pan-Orthodox unity which often takes form of a practical help wherever needed. Being a Cypriot Greek, that is, a son of a proud, hard-working nation imbued with genuine Orthodox tradition reflected in its everyday life, a nation that has had its share of opression and persecution, and being the Abbot of the Monastery that gave spiritual birth to Archbishop Makarios of Cyprus, he is very sensitive to any signs of injustice, whether they happen in the world or even within the Holy Church of Christ. Therefore, may this work of his help to bring some light into the challenging processes and ecclesial misconceptions that make many of our brothers and sisters in Christ, faithful sons and daughters of their Ukrainian church and homeland, united around their Metropolitan Onuphry in faith, hope and love, suffer on an everyday basis, while the "powerful of this world" keep their silence.

+JURAJ, Archbishop of Michalovce and Košice
Orthodox Church of the Czech Lands and Slovakia